Walk with Me, Jesus

A Widow's Journey

Walk with Me, Jesus

A Widow's Journey

Ronda Chervin, Ph.D.

With Heidi Hess Saxton

Foreword by Johnnette S. Benkovic

This is a derivative work of two books by Ronda Chervin, originally entitled A Widow's Walk (published by Our Sunday Visitor) and Weeping with Jesus.

Published by Simon Peter Press, Inc. PO Box 2187, Oldsmar, FL 34677

    08   09 10 11 12 13 10 9 8 7 6 5 4 3 2 1

Printed in the United States of America

ISBN 10: 0-9777430-3-9
ISBN 13: 978-0-9777430-3-2

For the First Dedicated Widows of the Holy Family:
Magdalena, Doreen, Marilyn, Dolores, Diane, and Marion

TABLE OF CONTENTS

FOREWORD
by Johnnette S. Benkovic

A Grief Shared

In April 2007, my daughter and I sought a ten-day respite on a sunny west coast Florida beach. It had been a difficult three years. We both needed time to heal and recuperate, and I knew I needed time to pray: specifically for discernment, wisdom, and guidance.

Earlier that month, my husband of nearly thirty-four years died of a Glioblastoma Multiforme IV brain tumor. Anthony's diagnosis had come just one year after our 25-year-old son had been killed in a vehicular accident soon after returning from serving his country in Iraq. My life had changed remarkably, and widowhood loomed large before me. If I were to meet this new challenge with faith, I knew I needed holy wisdom and guidance. Only in and through God could I find the treasury of grace packaged in the wrappings of my suffering.

Would I discover God's will for me as I made retreat with Him on that sunny shore? This was the question I asked, and its answer was the hope of my heart.

Anthony and I had experienced and witnessed abundant blessings through our crucible of suffering. Though it had been an intensely difficult time, it was a time robust with God's grace. We learned, in stunning ways, that His grace is always sufficient; that He is in the midst of all things; that His perfect plan is worked out in inexplicable and yet comprehensible ways; that everything He permits can be used to unite us more closely to Him; that Our Blessed Mother holds us in her immaculate heart; and that the Cross, when embraced, becomes a doorway to joy.

These were costly lessons to learn, and lessons I prayed to apply to my new state in life. I took a few prayer "tools" with me to my beachside retreat: my rosary, my Bible, the Divine Office, a copy of *Divine Intimacy* by Father Gabriel of St. Mary Magdalene, and writings on widowhood written by Ronda Chervin. As one day turned into another, I began to hear the voice of God speaking to me through these resources, offering me encouragement and insight, direction and hope.

I was especially edified by Ronda's writings. A widow herself, Ronda candidly shared her own struggle with widowhood and the challenges it presents. She told the stories of several holy women who became icons of triumph to me: St. Elizabeth Seton, Blessed Conchita, St. Jane de Chantal, Praxedes Fernandez, St. Rita of Cassia, and others. Some of these saintly women had immediate and pressing challenges to face – financial ruin, irascible relatives, small children to provide for, bitter and nearly inconsolable grief, the aftermath of painful and unhappy marriages, unusual circumstances and situations.

But each of them had learned a great lesson, a heavenly secret, a pearl of great price: they discovered how to make widowhood a pilgrim way to God, a path leading to sanctity and holiness, a sojourn into the abundant life of Jesus Christ. This was what I was after, this was what I was seeking, this was the cry of my heart. And from them I learned much.

I am so pleased that you, too, have an opportunity to meet these women through Ronda's book, *Walk With Me, Jesus*. This inspiring and introspective guide will lead you along the pilgrim path of widowhood. It will help you mine and discover the rich treasures of grace awaiting you along your way. It will offer you encouragement to persevere in the midst of sadness and sorrow, to hope in the midst of darkness and doubt, to trust in the midst of struggle and difficulty.

As Ronda reminds us, "Jesus does have the power to lift you, in a manner and time suitable to your own temperament, up to a new level of the Spirit, where your joy in him will be fuller."

May *Walk With Me, Jesus* be for you a source of comfort, consolation, wisdom, and hope. And may you discover, as I am doing, that God's grace is not only sufficient, it is infinite and will meet your every need.

Feast of St. Ignatius of Loyola
July 31, 2008

WALK WITH ME, JESUS ...

Lord, when the waves of pain threaten to engulf me ...
Draw me to the tranquil waters of Your peace.

When the rocks cause me to stumble and fall ...
Let Your light guide me safely along the path.

Lead me to the stillness, be my consolation,
Guide me to the haven of Your Sacred Heart.

In the name of the Father, and the Son,
and the Holy Spirit, Amen

INTRODUCTION

"Till death parts us." No matter how long ago you made this promise, in the end the vows resound in your head with crystal clarity. Circumstances do not change the finality of it. Whether your loss happened without warning, or was the final, inevitable conclusion of a prolonged period of suffering, death is as relentless as the tide.

The most amazing part of losing a spouse is that, somehow, life does go on. The flowers have wilted, the casserole dishes are washed and returned, the headstone has been set on the grave. The condolence cards have been taken from the mantle, and the thank-you notes that kept you busy during those first sleepless nights have been posted.

What happens next? The course ahead of you may still be unclear. And so, we begin this "widow's walk." This prayer journal will help you to draw from a rich treasury of spiritual graces: Scriptures, quotes from and stories about the saints, and other prayers and reflection questions that will lead you to draw closer to Jesus, our Second Bridegroom, and His mother, the Blessed Virgin Mary. She is a model for us, having experienced during her lifetime the loss of her beloved spouse.

❦ FOR PONDERING ❦

At this moment, what would you say are three concerns or questions pressing most urgently upon your heart?

_____

_____

_____

_____

_____

_____

_____

_____

_____

_____

_____

_____

❦ PRAYER OF THE DAY ❦

Mother Mary, you understand the soul-rending grief of widowhood. Pray for me now, that I might have the courage to face the challenges ahead. Help me to remain open to everything God wants me to learn in this new chapter of my life.

Heavenly Father, I abandon myself to Your boundless mercy. Give me strength to follow You, even when the way is hard to see. Thank You for all the ways You show Your love to me, especially ... [Name some of them here.]

_____

_____

_____

_____

_____

Chapter One

CRY OF INJUSTICE

The First Station
Jesus is Condemned to Death

Mary…

Your Son, who was to be judge of all the living and the dead, stood before a Roman judge and received an unjust sentence. Though you knew He was the "suffering servant" prophesied by Isaiah, did you wonder why He had to suffer this humiliation and in this way?

As widows, we sometimes question God's providence – and His love for us.

Why did that drunk driver who killed my husband survive?

Why did God permit that doctor's mistake?

Was there anything done – or left undone – that hastened the day or the hour?

Why did my husband have to die instead of me?

Holy Mary, pray for us … now and in the hour we cry for justice.

Jesus, You are the Lord of my life. I know that You permit only those things from which You can bring good. Help me to trust that even the day and the hour of my husband's death was known to You, and that he is enfolded in Your Sacred Heart now as then.

❦ FOR PONDERING ❦

What aspects of God's permissive will do I still find it difficult to accept in my grief?

❦ PRAYER OF THE DAY ❦

Walk with me, Jesus ... (insert your own prayer here)

Psalm 97:1-6

The Lord is king; let the earth rejoice
*   let the many isles be glad.*
Clouds and darkness are round about him,
*   justice and judgment are the foundation of his throne.*
Fire goes before him
*   and consumes his foes round about.*
His lightnings illumine the world;
*   the earth sees and trembles.*
The mountains melt like wax before the Lord
*   before the Lord of all the earth.*
The heavens proclaim his justice,
*   and all the peoples see his glory.*

🐚 FOR PONDERING 🐚

How does this passage speak to me today? How can I apply it to my life?

_____

_____

_____

_____

_____

_____

🐚 PRAYER OF THE DAY 🐚

Lord, I present myself to You. Today I choose to rejoice and to look for Your glory.

WHISPERS OF WIDOWHOOD: RONDA'S STORY

You have sent me misery and hardship,
but you will give me life again,
you will pull me up again from the depths of the earth,
prolong my old age, and once more comfort me.

Psalm 71:20-21
(The Jerusalem Bible)

I became a widow on October 9, 1993. I was fifty-six when my husband, Martin Chervin, died suddenly of cardiac arrest. He was seventy-four. At the time we were living in Woodland Hills, California, in an extended family home with one of my twin daughters, Carla; her husband, Peter; and two of our little grandsons, Nicholas and Alexander.

The prospect of becoming a widow was not new to me. After all, I had married a man nearly twenty years my senior; early in our marriage I had acknowledged the possibility that I might be a widow one day. However, Martin was a man with incredible vitality and *joie de vivre*. We always joked that, compared to him, I was the oldster because of my sedentary, professorial lifestyle.

Unfortunately, the reality was very different. Only a few years after our marriage in 1962, my husband developed a serious form of asthma. By 1968 he was semi-disabled. He could no longer devote himself to his work as an international book salesman; instead he spent the better part of each day writing original plays such as *Born/Unborn* (a pro-life play about the evils of abortion), *Myself: Alma Mahler* (a one-woman show about the marriage of Alma and Gustav Mahler), and his recently published masterpiece, *Children of the Breath* (about the dialogue of Christ and Satan in the desert). Because my husband was too ill to support the family, I worked full-time as a professor of Catholic philosophy. I loved my work, and expected to continue it in one form or another until my own death.

❦ FOR REFLECTION AND DISCUSSION ❦

In what ways were you and your husband complementary to each other? (Did your gifts correspond to his weaknesses, and vice versa?)

_____

_____

_____

_____

_____

_____

In what ways were you and your husband truly "partners"?

_____

_____

_____

_____

_____

_____

How have you experienced the truth of this passage from Psalms? _"You have sent me misery and hardship, but You will give me life again, You will pull me up again from the depths of the earth, prolong my old age, and once more comfort me."_

_____

_____

_____

_____

_____

_____

Blessed Marguerite d'Youville:
A Story of Patient Endurance

*"My dear Sisters, constantly remain faithful to the state which
you have embraced: always walk the paths of steadfastness,
obedience, and mortification—but above all, make the most
perfect union reign among you."*

Bl. Marguerite d'Youville

Blessed Marie-Marguerite d'Youville (d. 1771), born Marguerite Dufrost
de la Jemmerais, was one of six children born to parents of French ancestry
in Quebec, Canada. As a girl, Marguerite spent most of her time helping
her mother tend to her younger siblings.

The comfortable farming family was brought low by the death of her
father, but they lived as best they could off the land. As was the custom,
eleven-year-old Marguerite was sent to an Ursuline convent school; she was
unusually bright, and had a peaceful nature. Here Marguerite developed a
devotion to the Sacred Heart.

Though she was attracted to the religious life, Marguerite assumed
she would marry one day. The man her family picked for her, Francois
d'Youville, happened to be handsome and wealthy. Unfortunately the marriage turned out tragically. Francois was often gone on trading expeditions
that involved bribing the Indians to give up valuable furs for "fire water."

Equally difficult was Marguerite's domestic situation. Although she
was a creative and experienced homemaker, the young woman found
herself completely under the domination of a bitter, jealous mother-in-
law who resented the beauty, charm, and refined virtues of her son's wife.
To make matters worse, Marguerite's husband soon showed himself to be
crude, selfish, and indifferent. He left for long periods of time without
explanation, and was absent for the birth of their first child – busy trading
liquor for furs.

She wept bitter tears when she realized how difficult her situation was
to be, but she made up her mind never to criticize him, even though his
behavior became more and more ignoble. Her misery was compounded

when their infant son died. She gave the next child her husband's name, hoping that this would soften his heart. But he was also absent for this boy's birth and baptism. Their little girl, Marie, died as a baby; the next child, Louise, lived less than three months.

After the death of his mother, Francois gave himself up to a completely dissipated life of drinking, carousing, and gambling. He squandered all the family money, leaving Marguerite to work hard to provide for necessities. She also had to endure the disgust of the people of Montreal, enduring their sneers and reproaches when she stepped out with her baby to go to the marketplace.

Desperately Marguerite tried by prayer and example to convert her husband, lest his soul be damned for eternity. The future saint took solace in joining the Confraternity of the Holy Family, in this way taking as her own the family of Jesus, Mary, and Joseph. Under the guidance of a fine priest she learned how to sanctify the pain of her life day by day. The priest predicted that God would accomplish a great work through her one day.

Marguerite's husband died suddenly from inflammation of the lungs. The young widow requested that the priests of the Church offer three hundred sixty Masses for his soul. In spite of his abusive behavior, she grieved his death. Destitute and burdened with debts, Marguerite was left with two children — one aged six, the other a baby. (The last child, Charles, eventually became a priest.)

❦ FOR PONDERING ❦

"But whatever gains I had, these I have come to consider a loss because of Christ. More than that, I even consider everything as a loss because of the supreme good of knowing Christ Jesus my Lord. For his sake I have accepted the loss of all things and I consider them so much rubbish, that I may gain Christ and be found in him, not having any righteousness of my own based on the law but that which comes through faith in Christ…"

Philippians 3:7-10

Marguerite endured great suffering within her marriage, including the loss of three young children. Her husband's bad choices caused her other losses – loss of security, social standing, and financial hardship. Yet she forgave her husband. What about this story speaks to you, especially in light of the passage above?

_____

_____

_____

_____

_____

_____

_____

_____

_____

_____

☙ PRAYER OF THE DAY ☙

Lord Jesus, as I am stripped of all that once mattered to me,
help me to embrace more of You.

Psalm 10:10-14

*The helpless are crushed, laid low; they fall into the power of the
wicked,*
   *Who say in their hearts, "God pays no attention, shows no
concern, never bothers to look."*
   Rise up, LORD God! Raise your arm! Do not forget the poor.
   *Why should the wicked scorn God, say in their hearts, "God
doesn't care"?*
   *But you do see; you do observe this misery and sorrow; you take
the matter in hand. To you the helpless can entrust their cause; you
are the defender of orphans.*

❦ FOR PONDERING ❦

Do you ever feel as though the whole world has forgotten you and your
family? Have even your closest friends returned to "normal" life, or (worse)
urged you to get on with your life, as though you could outrun your grief?

The Lord sees you; He observes your misery and sorrow. Listen to the
words of Isaiah …

But Zion said, "The Lord has forsaken me; my Lord has forgotten me."
Can a mother forget her infant,
   or be without tenderness for the child of her womb?
Even should she forget, I will never forget you.
See, upon the palms of my hands I have written your name…
                                                    Isaiah 49:14-15

How does this passage apply to my life today?

_____

_____

_____

_____

_____

_____

_____

_____

_____

❦ PRAYER OF THE DAY ❦

"Lord, You do see; You do observe this misery and sorrow. You take the matter in hand. To You the helpless can entrust their cause; You are the defender of orphans and widows. Jesus, I trust in you."

PSALM 1
TREE BY A LIVING STREAM

Happy those who do not follow the counsel of the wicked,
Nor go the way of sinners, nor sit in company with scoffers.

Rather, the law of the LORD is their joy;
God's law they study day and night.

They are like a tree planted near streams of water,
that yields its fruit in season;

Its leaves never wither; whatever they do prospers.

But not the wicked! They are like chaff driven by the wind.

Therefore the wicked will not survive judgment,
nor will sinners in the assembly of the just.

The LORD watches over the way of the just,
but the way of the wicked leads to ruin.

ᑦ FOR REFLECTION AND DISCUSSION ᑦ

"Happy those who do not follow the counsel of the wicked, nor go the way of sinners, nor sit in company with scoffers." What does this say about how our friends influence us, for better or worse?

_____

_____

_____

_____

_____

_____

_____

_____

_____

"Like a tree planted near streams of water, that yields its fruit in season…"
Consider your current circumstances. What is your "living stream?" How do you see it bringing you life? What is your "fruitful field?"

_____

_____

_____

_____

_____

_____

_____

_____

_____

St. Rita of Cascia:
Patroness of the Impossible

"Why art thou proud, O dust and ashes? Dost thou forget that a God humiliated and annihilated Himself, stooping from Heaven to lift you thither?"

St. Rita of Cascia
Meditating on the Incarnation

She was born in 1381 to a couple that had prayed twelve years for a child. Despite her devotion to the Sacred Heart, the girl's life took a tragic turn when her parents determined that Rita would marry Paul de Ferdinand, a handsome but quarrelsome young man. In addition to his mean streak, Paul also drank and was known to seek out the company of immoral women. Rita objected to this marriage because of her dedication to the Lord, but her parents would not listen to her entreaties and prayers.

Their marriage from the beginning was an unhappy one. Rita's husband came home later and later at night, bruised and cut up from bouts of drunken brawling. The women of the neighborhood were amazed that Rita never spoke ill of Paul, even though she was visibly battered. Instead, Rita waited up to offer her husband late dinners. Paul responded with temper tantrums, throwing things around the house. Determined to help her husband reform, Rita persisted in turning the other cheek, praying for him, and doing penance for the salvation of his soul, especially by fasting.

Gradually Paul began to change, impressed by the goodness of his wife and also because she was expecting a child that turned out to be twin boys. Paul was changed by his fatherhood, but the boys evidently inherited their father's violent streak. When his sons were in their teens, Paul was ambushed and killed by an old enemy.

A friend told Rita that her husband forgave his assassin as he lay dying. But the sons, influenced by a pervasive culture of vengeance and their own fiery tempers, vowed to avenge their father's murder. Rita prayed that God would keep her sons from taking vengeance, and God answered that prayer. Her boys both died in an epidemic, despite her best efforts to save them.

As a widow as well as a grieving mother, Rita was grieved still further upon learning that she was not going to be received into Saint Mary Magdalene, the monastery she wished to enter. Even though she was well-known for her virtue and piety, in those days only young girls were being admitted to religious orders. Three times Rita applied; three times she was denied. Despite this, Rita remained convinced that God wanted her in this particular monastery, and increased her prayer. Meanwhile the forty-year-old widow stripped herself of her belongings so as to be ready to enter at a moment's notice.

The manner in which God chose to convince the mother superior and the sisters was totally miraculous. One night Rita heard a voice calling her name. A man who resembled pictures of John the Baptist was at the door. He led her out to a high mountain in the dark. There she met Saint Augustine and Saint Nicholas of Tolentino. She seems to have gone into a trance, and was discovered the next morning inside the closed and barred gates of the monastery of Saint Mary Magdalene; the sisters found her inside the chapel, seated in one of the stalls of the nuns.

The mother superior was furious when she realized it was Rita, the widow she had three times refused. The sisters as well as the superior finally had to see the hand of God in such a miraculous occurrence.

On the night before she professed her vows, the middle-aged nun had a dream. Christ appeared to her holding up an immense ladder reaching into heaven. When she awoke, Rita decided that she would need to climb the spiritual ladder to holiness step by step.

According to the Augustinian rule of that time, a cloistered sister could venture outside the enclosure to help the poor of the city. Saint Rita loved to wait on the steps of the monastery for the sick and poor to come so she could minister to them. In this way she became quite well known to the townspeople of Cascia.

One of the first recorded miracles attributed to God's grace working through the widow-saint concerned an old, barren twig of deadwood. The superior insisted that Rita drag buckets of water each day to make a dry twig grow. This was to be a test of her obedience. To the amazement of sisters in the convent, who doubted the older woman's holiness, after many days the twig began to turn green. Eventually delicious grapes grew on the vine that sprouted from the twig.

After Rita's death, many came for the last time to see the body of a woman they already revered as a saint. A relative with a paralyzed arm was instantly healed, as was a woodworker whose disabled hand had prevented him from making her coffin. Healed immediately, he was able to make the required wooden coffin. Soon the line of pilgrims increased as the people begged the intercession of Saint Rita, called the Saint of the Impossible.

In 1628, after the institution of a scrupulous investigation of claims regarding "so-called saints," Saint Rita was beatified following a two-year study; she was canonized in 1900 after even more careful research had been conducted. Her body remains intact, and lies in state in a basilica.

Throughout the centuries, miracles have taken place in Cascia. People come from all over the world with petitions to Saint Rita, whose little house is now a chapel. Near both the basilica and chapel are orphanages for girls and boys — so Saint Rita is still a mother, even from heaven.

☙ FOR PONDERING ☙

"Why art thou proud, O dust and ashes? Dost thou forget that a God humiliated and annihilated Himself, stooping from Heaven to lift you thither?"

St. Rita endured many unspeakable hardships in her marriage. She was often misunderstood and rejected as a religious sister as well. How does her story speak to you?

❦ PRAYER OF THE DAY ❦

Mother Mary, pray for me. When my happiness was threatened, when my loved ones suffered and struggled in the throes of death, as my mother your heart broke for me. Even now, as I continue to wander in fearsome darkness, you are with me still. St. Rita is remembered as the patroness of impossible causes; join your prayers with hers and mine, that our petitions would not go unheeded. Help me to find joy and consolation even in the midst of tears. Blessed Virgin, Faithful Widow, remember me.

CHAPTER TWO

CRY OF SEPARATION

Second Station
Jesus Accepts the Cross

Mary...

Many of us spent long hours at the bedside of our husbands, anticipating the separation that would come. Others of us experienced the tragedy of our spouse's sudden, unexpected death.

Just as nothing you could have said would have persuaded Jesus to evade the cross, we had no choice but to accept what we could not change.

The heaviness of that cross drained us, even as we persevered in hope.

Holy Mary, pray for us, that with each passing day this temporary separation will lead to everlasting joy.

Jesus, You endured all the trials we face, up to and including that final, wooden cross. You are with us every moment, in the pain and up to those final moments of our husband's earthly life.

Then and now, You want us to rest our weary heads in Your lap so that You can console us ... but we are too busy coping to come to You. As we look upon the second station and see You accepting Your cross, let us also see that You were holding us up through the intensity of our pain and loss.

❦ FOR PONDERING ❦

The Scriptures tell us that not even death "shall separate us from the love of God" (Romans 8:39). How does this apply to my situation?

_____

_____

_____

_____

_____

_____

❦ PRAYER OF THE DAY ❦

Walk with me, Jesus ... (insert your own prayer here)

_____

_____

_____

_____

_____

_____

Romans 8:35-39

What will separate us from the love of Christ?
   Will anguish,
   or distress,
   or persecution,
   or famine,
   or nakedness,
   or peril,
   or sword?

As it is written:

   "For your sake we are being slain all the day;
   we are looked upon as sheep to be slaughtered."

No, in all these things we conquer overwhelmingly through him who loved us. For I am convinced that …
   neither death, nor life,
   nor angels, nor principalities,
   nor present things, nor future things,
   nor powers,
   nor height, nor depth, nor any other creature
   will be able to separate us from the love of God in
      Christ Jesus our Lord.

⚘ FOR PONDERING ⚘

Have you been feeling "cut off" from those around you ... even from God, at times?

Tell God about it. He understands. Don't be afraid.

Feelings are fleeting. Feelings are not facts. Hold on to the truth of God's Word: *Nothing* can separate us from God's love. No one can pull us from the loving, prayerful gaze of our Blessed Mother.

Complete this thought: "I do feel close to God and my loved ones when ..."

_____

_____

_____

_____

_____

_____

⚘ PRAYER OF THE DAY ⚘

Walk with me, Jesus, when ... [fill in the rest of your prayer here].

_____

_____

_____

_____

_____

_____

A Heart in the Clouds

"On my bed at night I sought him whom my heart loves –
I sought him but I did not find him…"
Song of Songs 3:1

For the Christian couple, the separation death brings is only temporary … and yet the pain runs sharp and undeniably penetrating. When her husband Ludwig (Louis) died, Saint Elizabeth of Hungary wept bitterly for days. Saint Jane de Chantal was prostrate with grief for four months over the accidental death of her husband. She had great difficulty forgiving the hunter, who mistook Jane's husband for an animal he was hunting in the forest, and shot him.

A few months after her husband's death, Saint Elizabeth Seton wrote the following to a friend: "I have been to my dear husband's grave and wept plentifully over it with the unrestrained affection which the last sufferings of his life, added to remembrance of former years, had made almost more than precious …"

She writes about visiting a museum and loving the masterpieces of art, and feeling "alone but half enjoyed" herself, since she missed so much the joy her husband would have had in pointing things out to her. After one excursion she wrote to this same friend: "My poor heart was in the clouds, roving after my William's soul and repeating, 'My God you are my God, and so I am now alone in the world with you and my little ones, but you are my Father and doubly theirs.'"

❦ FOR PONDERING ❦

"My poor heart was in the clouds roving …" observed St. Elizabeth Seton. Where has your heart been roving lately?

_____

_____

_____

_____

_____

_____

_____

_____

_____

❦ PRAYER OF THE DAY ❦

You are my God … and I feel so alone as I wander these empty halls late at night. Please walk with me, Jesus. Holy Mary, Exalted Widow, stay beside me through the night.

St. Elizabeth Seton:
A Journey of Faith

"I have invariably kept in the background and avoided even reflecting voluntarily on anything of the kind knowing that Almighty God alone could effect it if indeed it will be realized.... God will in his own time discover his intentions, nor will I allow one word of entreaty from my pen — His...blessed Will be done."

St. Elizabeth Seton
In correspondence dated 1808.

In 1774 the first American-born saint was born to a prominent Episcopalian family of New York City. Elizabeth was only three years old when her mother died; she became much attached to her doctor father, Richard, and often accompanied him to Ellis Island, where he helped the sickly poor immigrants who had just arrived in the "Promised Land."

Elizabeth was unusually devout and loved to pray, living from Sunday to Sunday for her spiritual enrichment. Yet the young woman was subject to despairing, even suicidal, moods over the evils of the world and her own miseries.

Elizabeth married a charming young businessman, William Seton, and they had five children. Her happy family life was marred when her husband's business began to fail, leaving the family nearly bankrupt. This anxiety was compounded when her spouse contracted tuberculosis. Hoping to save the life of her beloved husband, Elizabeth decided to take a trip with him and their eldest daughter to Leghorn (or Livorno), Italy, which was supposed to be a better locale for a person with his health problems. Unfortunately, William's health worsened on the long journey. He was quarantined in an Italian lazaretto, and died about six weeks later.

This tragic loss was to become a source of blessing; the family of Antonio Filicchi, her husband's Italian business associate and a devout Catholic, helped Elizabeth and her daughter during this bleak time.

The faith of her hosts had a profound impact on Elizabeth. When she returned to New York, Elizabeth was torn between the church of her family and the Church she was becoming convinced had the greater claim to truth. Her family made it clear where her allegiance should be; they told her that if Elizabeth became a Roman Catholic, she would lose all the support from her Episcopalian relatives – support she needed as a poor widow. Nevertheless, the widow converted, trusting God for her physical needs.

As a Catholic, the previously wealthy widow found herself in comparative poverty. She embraced the opportunity to live simply, and to do the housework that a woman of her background would have had servants to perform. She was happy to be free of social obligations she had never really liked in the first place. Yet her life was also touched by sorrow again and again; she lost both her daughters as well as another relative who had converted to the Catholic faith because of her influence. These sufferings made Elizabeth's heart full of empathy. Consider the tone of a letter written to Cecilia, her convert relative who later joined her in the order, who was suffering persecution at the hands of the New York City family members:

"Yes, my Cecilia favored of Heaven, Associate of Angels, beloved Child of Jesus — You shall have the Victory, and He the Glory. To him be Glory forever who has called you to so glorious a combat, and so tenderly supports you through it. You will triumph, for it is Jesus who fights — not you my dear one — Oh so young and timid, weak, and irresolute, the Lamb could not stem a torrent, nor stand the beating storm — but the tender Shepherd takes it on his shoulder, casts his cloak about it, and the happy trembler finds itself at home before it knew its journey was half finished — and so my dear one it will be with you, He will not leave you one moment, nor suffer the least harm to approach you, not one tear shall fall to the ground nor one sigh of love be lost — happy, happy child — and if you are not removed to the sheltering fold that awaits you [in Elizabeth's home-convent-to-be] he will make you one in his own bosom until your task is done...how must [the saints] rejoice over you while walking so steadfastly in their paths, and their sufferings.

❦ FOR REFLECTION AND DISCUSSION ❦

*"From now on a household of five will be divided, three against two
and two against three; a father will be divided against his son and a
son against his father, a mother against her daughter and a daughter
against her mother, a mother-in-law against her daughter-in-law
and a daughter-in-law against her mother-in-law"*

(Luke 12:50-53).

St. Elizabeth experienced the truth of this passage many times in her own
life. Have you?

_____

_____

_____

_____

If so, how have religious divisions and conflicts affected you and your family
in the grieving process?

_____

_____

_____

_____

If not, how has your faith sustained you and your family members?

_____

_____

_____

_____

❦ PRAYER OF THE DAY ❦

When burdens threaten to crush me, when isolation overwhelms, You, oh Lord, have not abandoned me. Jesus, I trust in You.

St. Elizabeth Seton:
A Work of Charity

Trust in the Lord with all your heart,
on your own understanding rely not;
In all your ways be mindful of him,
and he will make straight your paths.
Proverbs 3:5-6

Although Elizabeth loved the sacramental and devotional life of the Roman Catholic Church, she was surprised that there was so little educational opportunity for children. She dreamed of starting her own little school for the poor. Eventually the widow's hopes were met with a similar idea on the part of the highly educated Bishop John Carroll of Baltimore. He invited her to start a teaching order for girls called The Sisters of Charity of Saint Joseph.

Elizabeth insisted that the bishop arrange things so her sons could be provided for at a flourishing Catholic school for boys, and her daughters could stay with her. The curriculum of the first school run by the newly formed order included reading, writing, arithmetic, English, French, and needlework. Quite a number of the students were boarders, so Elizabeth was busy from five-thirty in the morning until nine at night.

By no means was the way smooth for the new congregation of sisters. By 1809 Mother Seton was writing to Bishop Carroll of the difficulties. A cleric had ordered them to give up the direction of a priest who was greatly beloved for his understanding and inspiration. Instead they were to be ordered about by a superior they thought did not enter into the spirit of their own plans. Saint Elizabeth was willing to accept for herself the cross of the many misunderstandings that took place at the beginning of the foundation, but was not ready to see her sisters suffer.

For a while, another sister was appointed to head the order, which was followed by much turmoil. Elizabeth was especially anxious to retain charge over her own children under the new circumstances. Finally, the sister appointed as the congregation's head left, and the spirituality of the sisters grew in peace and joy."

Observe the sweet ironic humor of this account of the community Elizabeth wrote to her dear spiritual friend Antonio Filicchi, who helped the order financially as well as by his prayers:

> *"Now then you will laugh when I tell you that your wicked little Sister is placed at the head of a Community of Saints, ten of the most pious Souls you could wish, considering that some of them are young and all under thirty. Six more postulants are daily waiting till we move in a larger place to receive them, and we might be a very large family if I received half who desire to come, but your Reverend Mother is obliged to be very cautious for fear we should not have the means of earning our living during the Winter. Yet as Sisters of Charity we should fear nothing...."*

❦ FOR PONDERING ❦

Do you have a task at hand that seems too great to handle, a task that only seems to underscore the empty spaces in your life?

_____

_____

_____

_____

_____

_____

_____

Is God using the death of your husband to bring to life some new work through you? Or is it possible that God might now be calling you to a new path or a new endeavor?

What might it be? Write about it.

_____

_____

_____

_____

_____

_____

_____

🍂 PRAYER OF THE DAY 🍂

Almighty God,

Somehow, life moves on – even after the most devastating losses. There are still places to go, things to do, bills to pay … the list is endless, and my resources are few. Help me, Lord, to know where my priorities should be. In the name of the Father, and the Son, and the Holy Spirit. Amen.

Psalm 16:1-9

I love the LORD, who listened to my voice in supplication,
*   Who turned an ear to me on the day I called.*
I was caught by the cords of death;
*   the snares of Sheol had seized me; I felt agony and dread.*
Then I called on the name of the LORD, "O LORD, save my life!"
Gracious is the LORD and just; yes, our God is merciful.
The LORD protects the simple; I was helpless, but God saved me.
Return, my soul, to your rest; the LORD has been good to you.
For my soul has been freed from death, my eyes from tears,
*   my feet from stumbling.*
I shall walk before the LORD in the land of the living.

❧ FOR PONDERING ❧

"I was caught by the cords of death ..."

David, the warrior king, knew what it was to face death. As widows, we face this enemy more intimately, profoundly. Take a moment to meditate on this psalm, and journal about it.

_____

_____

_____

_____

_____

_____

_____

_____

❦ **PRAYER OF THE DAY** ❦

Lord,

When the grip of my memories rise up and threaten to overwhelm me, You have always been there to hold me steady. Thank You for never letting me walk alone.

LONGING AND SILENCE

Fear and trembling come upon me, and horror overwhelms me,
And I say, "Had I but wings like a dove, I would fly away and be at rest.
Far away I would flee; I would lodge in the wilderness.
I would hasten to find shelter from the violent storm and the tempest...

Psalm 55:6-9

In *By Grief Refined,* Alice von Hildebrand speaks of her own experiences when she writes:

[Think of] the widow whose human life was anchored in her spouse, and whose existence has been shattered by his death ... the loss of the person who was, humanly speaking, the sun of her earthly existence.

It is a terrible thing to wake up in the morning, stretch one's hand to caress the hand of the beloved, and grasp the void. To fall asleep is difficult – one's mind seems to be spinning, one's heart is restless, one's will is frozen.... We try desperately to wind back the clock, hoping to see him one more time, hear his voice one more time, tell him one more time that we love him and the bitter words come to our lips: "Never, never again."

Perhaps you can identify. You feel as if you died, too ... a spiritual death that testifies to the strength of the bond that united the two of you, and to the depth of your sorrow. Since death is the separation of soul and body, it is not surprising that by being torn away from the person with whom we were one flesh, a part of us dies as well.

How can people who do not believe in God or the immortality of the soul, bear this loss? For the Christian widow, the loss is still hard to bear – and yet the precious water of your tears irrigates a rich harvest of new life.

Your beloved remains mysteriously close in silence. Every time you wake up to find nothingness, you repeat to yourself, "No, I know that he is still there. He is invisible, but he is more loving than ever. I must now learn a new language, a new way of communicating with him."

You will never get over it. But in time you will know that love is stronger than death.

❦ FOR PONDERING ❦

"By being torn away from the person with whom we were one flesh, a part of us dies as well." Have you experienced this? When and how?

_____

_____

_____

_____

_____

_____

"Love is stronger than death."
In what ways and at what times do you feel closest to your husband?

_____

_____

_____

_____

_____

_____

_____

❦ PRAYER OF THE DAY ❦

Come Holy Spirit,
inspire me to speak words wise,
encouraging and consoling.
Jesus, Bridegroom of Widows help me.
Mary, Exalted Widow help me.
Widow saints, help me.

St. Elizabeth of Hungary: Like a Bending Willow

"Is that the secret of fruitful widowhood?
To bend like a willow with adversity
until we can stand strong again in the Lord?"
Said of St. Elizabeth of Hungary

One of the most famous young widow-saints was Elizabeth of Hungary (1207-1231). As an infant, Elizabeth was betrothed to Louis of Thuringia. At four years of age she was taken in procession to Thuringia to be prepared for her future life as a queen.

But the little girl was not at all the "princess type." Serious and prayerful, she was ridiculed by adults in the court. Happily, the one person who totally understood her was her future spouse, for he was the same way. Together the young people dreamed of the great deeds they could do for Christ when they grew up. They married when he was twenty-one and she was fourteen. They loved each other deeply, and spent many hours in prayer together.

When Louis died in a Crusade, Elizabeth wailed for days. "Dead! Henceforth all earthly joys and honors are dead to me!" she exclaimed. The death of Louis enabled his relatives to banish the hated pious princess, who disgusted them with her fanatical religious acts and whose generosity would impoverish them.

And so, immediately following her widowhood, Elizabeth knew poverty, homelessness, and persecution. All these trials she endured because of the simultaneous ecstatic mystical experiences she was enjoying. It was with gaiety that Elizabeth donned beggar's rags as she continued to serve the poor, with herself and her three children now also members of the class of the poorest.

The first night our widow-saint left the castle, she spent in a pigsty. Two faithful companions came with her. Delighted to finally be able to live like Saint Francis, Elizabeth rejoiced in her new freedom. Her biographer describes her as being like a willow growing by the riverside. When a flood comes, the willow bends. Undamaged, it straightens out after the flood. *Is that the secret of fruitful widowhood? To bend like a willow with adversity until we can stand strong again in the Lord?*

Finally the ex-princess was given a financial settlement from Louis' family. She established a hospital in Marburg, where she lived in small quarters. She was free now to nurse and care for the ill without worrying about her relatives' fears. In the sick she always saw the Lord.

The source of Saint Elizabeth's strength was her contemplative prayer and frequent reception of the Eucharist. Often she was seen with a shining face after receiving Communion. She described seeing the heavens open, and Jesus consoling her for all the sufferings of her life, making her entirely his.

At the age of twenty-four Saint Elizabeth died peacefully, surrounded by those who loved her, including a beggar child she had nursed from scurvy. At her death the singing of multitudes of birds could be heard, just as at the death of Saint Francis.

☙ FOR REFLECTION AND DISCUSSION ☙

Elizabeth's biographer described her as "a willow growing by a riverside, which bends with the flood, then straightens again." What metaphor would you use to describe yourself?

_____

_____

_____

_____

_____

_____

_____

Were there dreams you shared with your husband that you did not get to accomplish in his lifetime? Are there any of these dreams that died with him, which you would like to resurrect if you can?

_____

_____

_____

_____

_____

_____

_____

ॐ PRAYER OF THE DAY ॐ

St. Elizabeth:

You were of royal blood, born to take a role you could not choose for yourself. In good times and bad, you responded as best you could with courageous determination. Pray for me, that I might have a measure of this as well.

Chapter Three

CRY OF WEAKNESS

Third Station
Jesus Falls the First Time

Mary …

You saw your strong, manly son fall under the terrific weight of those beams. As you watched helplessly, waves of weakness filled your own body.

Did those feelings remind you of the grief you felt when Joseph died?

Watch over us, as our own physical strength dwindles slowly. Stay with us after the funeral, when we can hardly rise from our beds.

We, too, have felt those times of weakness that threatened to overtake us. Sometimes they linger still. Watch over us and lend us your strength and help us to move forward in hope.

Jesus, when widows collapse under the strain of early widowhood, You never chide us for failing to take up daily life tasks with our usual efficiency. Instead You remain at our side each day, and hover over our solitary beds, sending invisible graces. May we never doubt Your love for us as You bring new strength to our new state of life.

❦ FOR PONDERING ❦

When do I feel weakest and most in need of these divine graces?

_____

_____

_____

_____

_____

_____

❦ PRAYER OF THE DAY ❦

Walk with me, Jesus ... (insert your own prayer here)

_____

_____

_____

_____

_____

_____

_____

Feelings and Failings

*An unmarried woman or a virgin is anxious about the things of the
Lord, so that she may be holy in both body and spirit. A married
woman, on the other hand, is anxious about the things of the world,
how she may please her husband. …*

1 Corinthians 7:34

While my husband was still living, I had imagined that it would be much
easier to attain holiness when I was living on my own as a widow. Sadly,
this was not the case. The unholy faults of my nature – the chronic anger
over large and small frustrations, the manic talkativeness, and so on – did
not evaporate overnight.

My prayer life, which had gone into a sort of "dark night" after the
death of my son, did not radically improve after my husband's death. The
darkness turned to gray, with one or two beautiful moments each day; I
certainly did not experience the glowing radiance I had imagined it would
be … my single life of contemplative glory!

I had harbored romantic fantasies of meeting and marrying a wonderful
Christian man after Martin's death. Instead, I went through five immediate
rejections, and encountered seven more over the next two and a half years.
I seemed to scare men away when they found out I was available not as a
friend but as a potential spouse!

It is fun to write about these encounters with humor, but actually in
many of these cases I felt terrible pain, believing that each rejection was
proof that I was a hideous old bag, garrulous, annoying, and generally
impossible to view as an object of romantic love. No amount of loving praise
and comforting reassurances from family and friends seemed to heal these
feelings that got worse and worse as each attempt ended in failure. …

All along I undervalued the deep love my husband had for me,
discounted the way his virtues sustained me, and could not guess how
painful the loneliness of the single life really is, even with wonderful friends
surrounding me at every turn.

I did have an absolutely beautiful moment in prayer during which Jesus appeared to me in an inner vision in the form of El Greco's image of Christ in bridegroom garb. He told me that I belonged to him. I asked him if he wanted me to join a particular order of Sisters. He seemed to say: "Yes, that way you can focus on me alone." I was ecstatic about this; but my mentors all cautioned me, and, in fact, when I was with some aspirants of this order I felt not peaceful and good but claustrophobic.

☙ FOR PONDERING ☙

Can you relate to Ronda's experiences, at being surprised and even startled at times by the response of others to your widowhood? How about your own response to it?

☙ PRAYER OF THE DAY ☙

Lord,

When I am weak, make me strong by Your Spirit. When I feel unloved, help me to sense the depths of Your tender love and mercy. Amen.

So Tired…

They that hope in the Lord will renew their strength,
they will soar as with eagles' wings;
They will run and now grow weary,
walk and not grow faint.
Isaiah 40:31

Extreme fatigue is a well-known part of grieving. This is expressed by Elizabeth Seton, writing of the time when she was living alone with her five small children: "My woman [servant] has been again sick these five days I have been deprived of the dear morning visit of my Master — on Sunday I was so weak as not to be able to walk to town with my other fatigues…."

The husband of Conchita of Mexico died after they had been married for sixteen years and had parented nine children. In the days just before his death, Conchita writes:

"What struggles … what pains … what sufferings! This sword pierced my soul, without any assuagement, without any consolation…. Oh! If I had not been sustained by Him, then through my great weakness I would have succumbed! I saw, I affirmed, moment by moment, that my husband was losing his life … my heart was torn with pain…. To the measure that I saw our separation approaching, the tenderness of my heart toward him took on more and more considerable proportions. I felt I had no longer head, nor faith, nor reason, but only a heart. I experienced, as it were, horror for the spiritual life. What days I spent! What hours! What nights!"

☙ FOR PONDERING ☙

Have you been taking proper care of yourself? This may be especially difficult if you have children … but for their sake, you must tend to your own needs in order to have the resources you need to tend to theirs!

In what areas do you need to improve … and how do you intend to start?

_____

_____

_____

_____

_____

_____

_____

☙ PRAYER OF THE DAY ☙

Blessed Widow,

In the days following the death of your husband – and even more so, after the death of your Son – it must have been a struggle to manage even the simplest tasks. You understand what I am going through. Pray for me, then, with your empathetic heart, that my way will be clear for me.

PSALM 6

Have pity on me, LORD, for I am weak;
heal me, LORD, for my bones are trembling.

In utter terror is my soul-- and you, LORD, how long...?

Turn, LORD, save my life; in your mercy rescue me.

For who among the dead remembers you?
Who praises you in Sheol?

I am wearied with sighing; all night long tears drench my bed;
my couch is soaked with weeping.

My eyes are dimmed with sorrow, worn out because of all my foes.

Away from me, all who do evil! The LORD has heard my weeping.

The LORD has heard my prayer; the LORD takes up my plea.

My foes will be terrified and disgraced; all will fall back in sudden
shame.

❦ FOR PONDERING ❦

"I am wearied with sighing; all night long tears drench my bed..." Have you noticed any changes in how your grief manifests itself? Do tears come unexpectedly, without warning? Do you find it difficult to cry at all ... even when others seem to expect it?

How would you describe your feelings of grief at this time? Remember, there are no right or wrong answers. Though the "phases" of grief are common to many, the experience of how those phases are lived out is unique to the individual.

_____

_____

_____

_____

_____

_____

৩ PRAYER OF THE DAY ৩

Write your own paraphrase of this psalm as your prayer to God.

_____

_____

_____

_____

_____

_____

_____

_____

WIDOWS IN SCRIPTURE:
AN OVERVIEW

"When brothers live together and one of them dies without a son, the widow of the deceased shall not marry anyone outside the family; but her husband's brother shall … [marry her.] The first-born son she bears shall continue the line of the deceased brother, that his name may not be blotted out from Israel."

Deuteronomy 25:5-6

"In the middle of the night, however, the man gave a start and turned around to find a woman lying at his feet. He asked, "Who are you?" And she replied, "I am your servant Ruth. Spread the corner of your cloak over me, for you are my next of kin."

Ruth 3:8-9

"A wife is bound to her husband as long as he lives. But if her husband dies, she is free to be married to whomever she wishes, provided that it be in the Lord."

I Corinthians 7:39

In her book entitled *The Widows: A Women's Ministry in the Early Church*, Bonnie Bowman Thurston observes that from the earliest times of Israel's history, support was given to widows. The Hebrew word for widow, *almanah*, is derived from the word *alem* meaning "unable to speak," related to a word meaning to be in pain. The sense is not that widows became mute, but that they were not spoken for.

In the Old Testament, for a husband to die before a still-fertile wife was considered to be a sign of retribution for sins. The widow shared a sense of being disgraced. This is reflected in the story of Naomi, Ruth's mother-in-law, who calls herself afflicted and bitter (Ruth 1:20-21).

A widow had various options. Her birth family could pay her purchase price to her husband's heirs, or she could remain in his family in a lowly status. She could remarry, but it was considered better to wait to marry a brother of her husband to ensure the male line.

A widow could not inherit, which is why she was to be the beneficiary of charity. In this way God protected her through the services of the community (Psalm 68:5; Proverbs 15:25). Men were commended who helped widows (Job 29:13). Those who mistreated widows were to be condemned in the Day of Judgment (Job 31:16, 28).

Some say that Jesus was especially sensitive to widows. He understood their needs and their concerns. He also understood their position in the culture of His day. Mary, His own mother, was a widow. His compassion toward the widow is reflected in His loving concern for her. The climax of this compassion is seen when He entrusts His mother to St. John as He hung from the cross. What love He displays for His mother and, through her, for all widows!

This providential concern is seen throughout the Gospel accounts. In the Gospel of Mark, we read of some leaders who devour widows' houses (Mark 12:38-40). Jesus honors the poor widow who put her last coin (a "mite") into the temple treasury (Mark 12:41-44; Luke 21:1-4). He saw her humble gift for what it was: a symbol of total self-giving and trust in Divine Providence.

The Gospel of Luke recounts the story of the widow of Nain (Luke 7:11-17), who was overcome with grief because her only son had died, depriving her of any legal protection. Later on (18:1-8), the story of the widow whose repeated entreaties wears out a judge was elevated to symbolize how God especially cares for those who pray with confidence.

In the teachings of Jesus, widows had a special place, representing a "new system of values breaking into the world." The widow becomes a shining example of how God "has put down the mighty from their thrones, and exalted those of low degree" (Luke 1:52).

🙂 FOR REFLECTION AND DISCUSSION 🙂

Who is your favorite Scripture widow, and why?

_____

_____

_____

_____

_____

_____

Read the accounts of the widows in the Gospel passages cited above. Which of the widow(s) do you most relate to and why? What is Jesus saying to you through her/their account?

_____

_____

_____

_____

_____

🙂 PRAYER OF THE DAY 🙂

Lord Jesus,

Throughout Your life and teachings, You exalted the widow as one who is uniquely dependant on God. As I ponder these Scriptures, teach me how I might grow in that trust and confidence. In You alone do I trust. Amen.

St. Brigid of Sweden: Discerning Good and Evil

"Three times I begged the Lord about this [thorn in the flesh], that it might leave me, but he said to me, 'My grace is sufficient for you, for power is made perfect in weakness.' I will rather boast more gladly of my weaknesses, in order that the power of Christ may dwell in me."

2 Corinthians 12:8-9

Saint Brigid was assisted by a priest-chaplain who stayed with her on her travels and in Rome. He served as her confessor, and brought the sacraments to all those Brigid managed to bring to conversion.

Besides friends on earth, Brigid also had heavenly helpers. When she was living in Rome, Saint Agnes taught her how to read Latin and speak it well enough to teach pilgrims from many lands. If Brigid had been able to speak only in Swedish, she could never have had the influence she did in Rome.

Nevertheless, Brigid was concerned at times about the origins of these supernatural interventions, wondering whether the visions and locutions were coming from Christ or from the Devil. Concerning how she was to discern, the Blessed Virgin told Brigid:

"Fear not that what you now see and hear has come from an evil spirit. For as the sun brings light and warmth, which the dark shadow does not bring, so the Holy Ghost, when it enters into the heart of a man, brings two things: the warmth of love and the light of faith. You feel these two now, and they do not go with the devil."

❦ FOR PONDERING ❦

Since becoming a widow, have there been times when you sensed that you were being given heavenly guidance, particularly in an area in which you felt weak or vulnerable? Write about it.

_____

_____

_____

_____

_____

_____

_____

❦ PRAYER OF THE DAY ❦

Dear Heavenly Father,

The thorns of grief and weakness prick my soul at times, but I thank You that I have not been forgotten or left to my own devices. Help me to lean on You, that everyone will see Your strength working through me. Amen.

Those who go down to the sea in ships,
   who do business on great waters;
They have seen the works of the LORD,
   and His wonders in the deep.
For He spoke and raised up a stormy wind,
   which lifted up the waves of the sea.
They rose up to the heavens, they went down to the depths;
   their soul melted away in their misery.
They reeled and staggered like a drunken man,
   and were at their wits' end.
Then they cried to the LORD in their trouble,
   and He brought them out of their distresses.
He caused the storm to be still,
   so that the waves of the sea were hushed.
Then they were glad because they were quiet,
   so He guided them to their desired haven.
Let them give thanks to the LORD for His lovingkindness,
   and for His wonders to the sons of men!
                                        Psalm 107:23-31

CHAPTER FOUR

CRY OF ABANDONMENT

Fourth Station
Jesus Meets His Mother

Mary …

As I meditate upon this station of the Cross, I am struck by what an unforgettable encounter this must have been between you and your Son. It reminds us that deeper even than shared joy is shared agony!

Pray for us now. Some of us looked into the eyes of our husbands as they left this world. Some had no chance to say goodbye – he died far away or instantaneously, without warning.

Pray for us, your abandoned daughters.

Jesus, You knew Your mother's heart inside out. Though it comforted You to receive her last touch and glance, it also must have grieved You to be the cause of her pain.

Thank You for the family, friends, priests, and parishioners who stayed with us as we made the way of the cross with our husbands. Even if no one walked with us, You, Jesus, Your mother, our angels and the widow saints were there.

Let us never be so frantic in our widowhood that we push away the love of those who reach out to us.

☙ FOR PONDERING ☙

Is there someone in your life that you've lost touch with, and with whom you feel the need to be reconnecting, even if it is difficult or awkward? What do you hope to gain from re-establishing this relationship?

_____

_____

_____

_____

_____

_____

_____

☙ PRAYER OF THE DAY ☙

Walk with me, Jesus ... (insert your own prayer here)

_____

_____

_____

_____

_____

_____

_____

STORMS OF EMOTION:
RONDA'S STORY

The year Martin died, our children were grown and we were enjoying our grandchildren. Our marriage had been flourishing with a closeness we had not experienced since courtship. The reason for this renewed sense of intimacy, however, was tragic. In 1991 when our nineteen-year-old son committed suicide, the agony drew us into much greater emotional and spiritual intimacy. An account of this period in my life can be found in my book *En Route to Eternity — The Story of My Life*.

Sadly, this kind of intimate connection, which characterized our last years together, had been largely missing from the rest of our marriage. Prior to our son's death, our marriage had been a rocky one. Because of this, I had always been afraid I might not be able to act as expected at the moment of his death. But that was not the case. Not only did I wail with grief, I even reverted to a biblical archetype, rending my dress as I rocked on the living room floor, holding my daughters in my arms.

During the first week I felt a peculiar, scary lightness. It was as if I were floating on the ceiling, like a balloon released from a rock to which it had been tied. This dizzying vertigo was still with me nearly three years into widowhood. My earthy husband had been the ground for my feet. Without him, I did not soar toward Christ: I just floated, miserable and without ballast! This lack of grounding took the form of severe anxiety attacks, which I sometimes experienced several times a day on anniversaries and holidays. I also suffered from chronic low feelings.

I had imagined for so long what widowhood would be like; the reality was something altogether different. I absolutely hadn't the faintest idea how horrible being a widow could be. I enjoyed enormously giving away many of our material possessions to family and friends, even before the funeral. I also gave away large sums of money to the poor out of my salary.

However, to my horror I discovered that this joy was not a permanent thing. Yes, I felt happy writing checks and giving things away, but the feeling did not last. The loss of my husband gnawed at me, making me utterly miserable!

❦ FOR PONDERING ❦

Have you experienced other losses since your husband's death? How has your grief for your husband affected your response to the subsequent loss?

_____

_____

_____

_____

_____

_____

_____

❦ PRAYER OF THE DAY ❦

My Jesus,

You allowed as part of your plan for me and for my sister-widows that we would go through this particular form of anguish. But your wish is not that we should die of anxiety, depression, or despair, but that we should receive your love as a second bridegroom, that like the widow-saints we may be joyful in the midst of suffering and true sisters to everyone we meet.

BLESSED CONCHITA:
DRINKING DEEP OF SORROW

The promises of the LORD are sure, silver refined in a crucible,
silver purified seven times.
Psalm 12:7

Many widows find that they get a much clearer picture of all their husband's virtues after death strips away the images of daily life that are neutral or mixed with the flaws of the same man. This is the bittersweet portrait Conchita drew of her own husband in her diary:

> *Here is a picture of what my husband was. He was very good, a Christian and a gentleman, honest, correct, intelligent and big-hearted. He was sensitive to adversity, full of tenderness toward me, an excellent father of a family, who had no other diversion than his children. They were his joy and he suffered greatly when they were ill... a homebody, very simple, filled with deference and delicacy. He had a strong, energetic character, which, as time passed, he toned down...from the day after our wedding until his death, he let me receive Communion every day...he had a great fear of death...before dying, he made a general confession and his fear of death changed into perfect acceptance of the divine will.*

So terrible was her grief during the first days of widowhood that the doctors thought she would die of it. "Even when I control myself," she wrote, "I go through moments of despondency. My tears flow very often without my being able to hold them back. My heart of flesh recalls many a sorrowful memory. I suffer, drinking deep of sorrow. May God be blessed for all!...The sound of my children crying over their father pierced my soul.... My body is exhausted. Now it is that I feel wearied.... May the Lord sustain me with His cross."

On the third anniversary of her husband's death Conchita wrote in her diary, "my heart struggles constantly. Truly, and literally, I water with my tears the bread I eat, the ground and my crucifix! Oh my Jesus! What You wish, that I wish too....I feel so awfully alone. Oh Mary, my Mother, have pity on me."

After twenty years, and then thirty years, she was praying constantly that Christ would fill her husband with his glory and "greet him for me."

❧ FOR PONDERING ❧

Which of your husband's qualities and habits do you miss most, or appreciate most, in his absence? In what ways did his example challenge you to cultivate virtue?

_____

_____

_____

_____

_____

_____

❧ PRAYER OF THE DAY ❧

Lord,

When I cannot feel Your hand, still Your mighty arms bear me up.
If I cannot hear Your voice, still You listen for my call.
Infinite Grace, infinite Mercy,
You, O Lord, are all in all to me.

Psalm 16:7-11

Pleasant places were measured out for me;
fair to me indeed is my inheritance.

I bless the LORD who counsels me;
even at night my heart exhorts me.

I keep the LORD always before me;
with the Lord at my right,
I shall never be shaken.

Therefore my heart is glad, my soul rejoices;
my body also dwells secure,

For you will not abandon me to Sheol,
nor let your faithful servant see the pit.

You will show me the path to life,
abounding joy in your presence,
the delights at your right hand forever.

ॐ FOR REFLECTION AND DISCUSSION ॐ

Create a personal timeline. Below the line, note painful milestones – the diagnosis, the loss of memories and/or functions, the moments when you as the caregiver struggled. (Don't worry about exact dates as much as the stages.) Above the line, note any bright spots you experienced … special ministrations of close friends and family, the good times and memories, times of peace or release of pain.

My Personal Timeline

Now go back and make little crosses along the places when you felt especially close to God, or felt that the prayers of others were sustaining you in a special way. What do you see?

❦ **PRAYER OF THE DAY** ❦

Write a prayer of thanksgiving for what you've learned.

_____

_____

_____

_____

_____

_____

_____

_____

_____

_____

THE STORY OF RUTH

Put away your misdeeds from before my eyes;
cease doing evil; learn to do good.
Make justice your aim: redress the wronged,
hear the orphan's plea, defend the widow.
Isaiah 1:17

While the Scriptures instruct the faithful to care for widows, it also reveals something important about these women: Both the Old and New Testaments include accounts of widows who played an important role in salvation history and in the early Church. These positive portraits are a welcome contrast to the somewhat negative societal images in many present-day cultures. We find in Scripture various passages about forlorn widows, heroic widows, and widows free for service to others in the early Church.

Let us look at the famous story of Ruth, the Moabite woman who married a son of Elimelech and Naomi after this couple had migrated and settled in Moab to escape famine.

After the death of her husband and two sons, Naomi journeyed back toward Judah, since the famine had ended. Both her daughters-in-law loved her and didn't want to live without her. However, Naomi thought it would be better for the young widows to seek husbands of their own culture.

The first daughter-in-law, called Orpah, left. The second, Ruth, clung to Naomi not only because she loved her mother-in-law, but also because she preferred the religion of Naomi's people. Ruth's declaration to her mother-in-law is often quoted in wedding ceremonies:

> *"... for where you go I will go, and where you lodge, I will lodge; your people*
> *shall be my people, and your God my God"* (Ruth 1:16).

Rereading these lines as a widow, I wonder if the way Ruth clung to her mother-in-law is indicative of how abandoned a widow can feel, and how much family can mean in such circumstances.

Naomi's desperation is reflected upon her return to Bethlehem, when she changes her name from Naomi (which means pleasant) to Mara (which means bitter, see Ruth 1:20-21). What follows is the well-known story of how the impoverished and widowed Ruth finds a husband in Boaz, a wealthy landowner, by gleaning in his fields. Long before he married her, Boaz had proven himself to be an honorable man because of the way he protected this young widow without father or brothers, recognizing her as a "woman of worth" (see Ruth 2:9, 3:11).

Boaz offers to buy the land of Naomi's former husband, thereby gaining the right to take Ruth as his own. Only when the community validated this right did he take Ruth as his wife. In due time she bore him a son, Obed, who became the father of Jesse, who was the father of David (Ruth 4:13-17), of whom Jesus was considered a direct descendant.

☙ FOR REFLECTION AND DISCUSSION ☙

The story of Ruth and Naomi has much to say about love. Identify the kinds of love the story portrays.

_____

_____

_____

_____

_____

_____

_____

_____

How does Boaz "prove" his love for Ruth? What character traits does he possess that shows him to be an honorable man?

_____

_____

_____

_____

_____

How did God provide for all parties in the story? What does this say to you about God's provision for you?

_____

_____

_____

_____

_____

❦ PRAYER OF THE DAY ❦

Dear Father God, there are so many places in the Bible where you exhort people to take care of the widows. We know you love us in a special way. As we review the stories of some of these widows, help us to avoid dangerous paths and follow good ones. Show us how to show your love and compassion to all lonely people, including divorced and single mothers.

Jesus, Second Bridegroom of Widows, help us,

Mary, Exalted Widow, help us. Widow saints, help us.

St. Jane de Chantal:
Abandoned to Family

"Those who do not like their widowhood are widows in appearance only, for their hearts are still married.... Praise God who has given you this precious, holy love [of Christ]; help it to grow more and more each day, and your own consolation will increase proportionately.... Avoid anxiety and worries, for nothing so impedes our progress toward perfection. Place your heart in our Lord's wounds gently, and not by force...."

Advice of St. Francis de Sales to St. Jane de Chantal

Jane de Chantal (1572-1641) was born to a noble family of Burgundy lawyers. Because her mother died when Jane was still young, most of her education took place at her father's side. From him she developed many analytical and administrative gifts.

At twenty, Jane married the Baron Christophe de Chantal. They enjoyed a most happy marriage and had six children, four of whom survived infancy. When her husband was killed in a hunting accident, Jane was devastated. For four months she was prostrate with grief, then decided to take a private vow of chastity.

Jane wanted to return to the house of her beloved father, but the only way to provide security and social advantages for her children was to move into the home of her father-in-law and his mistress with their five children.

Life in this household was most difficult for Jane. Her father-in-law's mistress, who was the housekeeper, tried to minimize the influence devout and insightful Jane had on Jane's father-in-law. The housekeeper/mistress was particularly irked by Jane's love of the poor and disenfranchised. Even so, during her seven years at the house, Jane managed to establish a kind of medical dispensary out of a wing of the manor house. So committed was Jane to tending the sick poor with her own hands, she herself contracted dysentery and became seriously ill. She recovered, but during this time was eaten up with the desire to do God's will. Her spiritual life was like an interior fire that burned ceaselessly, concealed by her sense of propriety, her practical activity, and her longing to please her loved ones.

While she yearned interiorly for a hidden, cloistered life of prayer, circumstances made it necessary for her to stay in the world. This was a difficult burden for Jane, but she was to develop a perfect obedience to the will of God, and pray for an increase in faith that her dream would come true in spite of all the human reasons to doubt. She was moved to exclaim: "I tried to offer God my heart completely emptied of any wish but his pure, chaste love and obedience to him."

Jane struggled with her husband's family, who wanted her to solve her own problems and those of her children by a financially advantageous second marriage. Jane resisted with all her strength. "As much as I was able, I clung to the wood of the Cross, lest so many sweet siren songs tempt my soul to go soft and yield to the world's attractions."

❦ FOR PONDERING ❦

Widows with children may have a tendency to idealize the solitary, contemplative life. De Sales wrote to his married sister:

> *"Let us all belong to God … in the midst of so much busyness brought on by the diversity of worldly things. Where could we give better witness to our fidelity than in the midst of things going wrong? Ah, dearest daughter, my sister, solitude has its assaults, the world its busyness; in either place we must be courageous, since in either place divine help is available to those who trust in God and who humbly and gently beg for His fatherly assistance."*

In what specific ways do I currently need to trust God and "humbly and gently beg for His fatherly assistance?" Write them down.

_____

_____

_____

_____

Note the columns below. If you are a single parent, what challenges are you facing right now? List them in the first column. In the second column, list the ways your children (or extended family) have been a source of comfort or spiritual strengthening to you.

Single Parenting Challenges	Single Parenting Blessings

ॐ PRAYER OF THE DAY ॐ

Heavenly Father,

I rely on your "fatherly assistance." In every circumstance of my life … in the solitude as in the chaos, in the good times and hard times, You are my anchor in the storm. Thank You for being a constant source of strength. Amen.

ST. FRANCES DE SALES AND ST. JANE DE CHANTAL: A "BOND OF PERFECTION"

"Francis and Jane are not two lonely people who cling to each other in order to find a safe home in the midst of a fearful world. Both of them have found Jesus as the Bridegroom of their souls. He is the fulfillment of all their desires. He himself makes their friendship possible. They have been given to each other as spiritual friends, to enjoy each other's spiritual gifts, to support each other in their commitment to faithfulness, to be of mutual help in their search for perfection and to give shape to a new spiritual family in the Church."

Henri J. Nouwen, from the preface of
Francis de Sales, Jane de Chantal:
Letters of Spiritual Direction

Perhaps no woman saint depended so much on the advice of a male saint as Saint Jane de Chantal depended on her mentor, Saint Francis de Sales. Before their auspicious meeting in 1604, some years after Jane became a widow, each had a vision from God of the physical form of the other with a conviction from the Holy Spirit that this was the person who would help most with the fulfilling of Christ's will.

In 1610, Jane left her family and moved to Annecy, the diocese where Francis de Sales was bishop, in order to form the new Order of the Visitation. At first Jane wanted to found an order that would be both contemplative and active — the sisters were to engage in works of charity during part of the day. Admission to the order would not depend upon criteria common in that time for other communities, such as youth, health, and freedom from all family ties. The Visitation was to be more like a home — simple and modest and ascetical, but always oriented to intimate love for God and for one another. They were to be gentle and tender, not so much occupied with great things but with doing little things with great love.

Saint Francis de Sales continued to advise St. Jane as she directed the new order; he recommended that Jane correct the sisters with affection and patience, without harshness or strong emotion. He inspired the Visitation community, who embodied his ideals for the spiritual life. He visited frequently to give sublime conferences, and took part in the most seemingly mundane decisions of the devout group under his direction. I especially love the understanding of our feminine nature that Saint Francis exhibited when he insisted that they make their habit a little more attractive. He said that he wanted them to be holy … but not hideous!

So closely were Jane and Francis joined in a "bond of perfection" that the holy priest could write Jane in all simplicity:

> *"I know you have complete confidence in my affection; I have no doubt about this and delight in the thought. I want you to know and to believe that I have an intense and very special desire to serve you with all my strength.... I believe it is from God.... Make the most of my affection and of all that God has given me for the service of your soul...."*

🕊 FOR PONDERING 🕊

"… Make the most of my affection and of all that God has given me for the service of your soul…"

In this context, the word "affection" has a connotation that is distinctly paternal (or fraternal), rather than romantic. Yet their bond was considered "perfect." What does this say to you about the complementarity of the sexes even within the context of a chaste friendship? And what of the dangers of misconstruing filial affection for something altogether different?

❧ **PRAYER OF THE DAY** ❧

O Sacred Heart of Jesus,
Drive me deep into that Ocean
Steep me in the Love
That will never let me go.

Safeguard my heart
From all that is not You,
And set my eyes with infinite care
Upon Your holy path.

When I feel abandoned,
Let me walk within that Garden
And feel that Holy Passion
So that I never want for more.

O Sacred Heart of Jesus,
Drive me deep into that Ocean
Steep me in the Love
That will never let me go.

CHAPTER FIVE

CRY OF NEEDINESS

Fifth Station
Simon Helps Jesus Carry the Cross

Mary …

You wished you could carry that cross for your Son. You must have sighed in relief to see Simon bearing the weight.

As widows, even after many years, we can feel lonely, overwhelmed, and hopeless, desperately wishing for help.

Holy Mary, pray for your daughters in our hour of need.

Jesus, You are the God-man, yet You let another help when You were unable to keep going. Why, then, should we be too proud to beg? So often a cry brings assistance that does not come to those who hide their weakness.

In the Scriptures, the Holy Spirit promises rewards to those who aid widows. Show us who can help us in our neediness…and, when there really is no one, let us always fall back on You, the Second Bridegroom of widows. Strengthen our backs even as the cross still weighs us down.

❦ FOR PONDERING ❦

What is weighing me down at this moment? Is God asking me to let go of pride, admit my need, and reach out to someone who would like to help?

_____

_____

_____

_____

_____

_____

❦ PRAYER OF THE DAY ❦

Walk with me, Jesus ... (insert your own prayer here)

_____

_____

_____

_____

_____

_____

_____

PRAXEDES FERNANDEZ:
A WIDOW'S MIGHT

"And looking on, he [Jesus] … saw also a certain poor widow casting in two brass mites. And he said: Verily I say to you, that this poor widow hath cast in more than they all: For all these have of their abundance cast into the offerings of God: but she of her want, hath cast in all the living that she had."

Luke 21:1-3, Douay-Rheims

A perfect example of a contemporary widow-saint who devoted herself to helping her own children and all needy persons she could minister to is the holy woman being considered for canonization: Praxedes Fernandez (1886-1936).

Born to a well to do but hardworking family in the mining district of Asturias, Spain, the child Praxedes was unusually pious. She was devoted to Christ and his Church and to the needs of the poor. By the age of eleven, she became her mother's right arm in housekeeping, running the store, and taking care of the garden. Educated briefly at a Dominican school, Praxedes practiced constant prayer in the midst of the duties of family life that were sufficiently plentiful to require her to interrupt her education.

She was reluctant to marry, but Praxedes finally accepted the proposal of Gabriel Fernandez, a simple laborer who worked in the mines. She was fond of him because of his basic goodness, even though he tended to be irascible. They had many children, and Praxedes enjoyed her hidden life as the wife of a worker. She used to say, "I wish I could be like those violets hidden in the weeds, but still giving off such a pleasing aroma." She had learned from the story of Saint Zita, a servant-saint, how to pray continually while doing menial tasks.

Praxedes' husband did not share his wife's spiritual fervor. He began objecting to how much time she spent in church. Once when she had been meditating on the Passion, he slapped her in the face. Praxedes never complained about his harsh treatment, but a neighbor went to his mother about it. Praxedes' mother-in-law was outraged, for she admired her son's wife very much. She saw to it that he never hurt Praxedes in this way again.

Sorrow came into the personal life of Praxedes with the death of her beloved father and then a freak train accident that killed her husband. Afraid that her spouse might have died in sin, she spent much time praying for his salvation and was eventually reassured that he was safe with the Lord.

At the death of her husband, Praxedes was left penniless with her four children. Praxedes decided to move in with her mother and an unmarried sister. In exchange for room and board, she was happy to cook, clean, garden, wash, and serve at the table. To provide some money for clothing for her children, as well as education, she took in sewing for others.

Visitors to the house were horrified to see Praxedes working so slavishly. But Praxedes' sister, an unmarried schoolteacher who disliked having children in the home, was so spiteful that she kept under lock and key the best food for herself, forcing Praxedes and her sons to dine separately on inferior food. Praxedes' friends were outraged, but Praxedes thought of these humiliations solely in supernatural terms, as crosses to offer to the Lord.

In spite of her many duties in the house, Praxedes always made time for Mass. She taught others "the time it takes to assist at Mass, far from being an impediment, serves to help you do them [chores] even better."

♥ PRAYER OF THE DAY ♥

Hear my cry for help, my king, my God! To you I pray, O LORD;
at dawn you will hear my cry; at dawn I will plead before you and wait.
Psalm 5:4-5

Read that passage again, slowly, as your heart-felt prayer. What sentiments or emotions well up within you? Entrust them to Our Lord.

_____

_____

_____

PSALM 27:8-10

"Come," says my heart, "seek God's face."
Your face, LORD, do I seek!

Do not hide your face from me;
do not repel your servant in anger.
You are my help; do not cast me off;
do not forsake me, God my savior!

Even if my father and mother forsake me,
the LORD will take me in.

🍃 FOR PONDERING 🍃

Is there a particular need weighing on your heart right now? Perhaps it is financial, or something altogether different. Do not be afraid to tell the One who loves you most.

_____

_____

_____

_____

_____

_____

What losses have you experienced – in addition to the companionship and
security of a spouse – that have been difficult to bear? Your King is listening,
ready to pour out His riches upon you … unexpected riches, such as you
never thought to ask Him for.

_____

_____

_____

_____

_____

_____

_____

Tell Him of your neediness. Tell Him of your loss.
Tell Him how He, your Second Bridegroom, is needed most.

❦ PRAYER OF THE DAY ❦

Walk with me, Jesus … [Insert your prayer here.]

_____

_____

_____

_____

_____

_____

_____

_____

A GOSPEL WIDOW:
"TABITHA, ARISE!"

"Now in Joppa there was a disciple named Tabitha [Dorcas].
She was completely occupied with good deeds and almsgiving.
Now during those days she fell sick and died, so after washing her,
they laid [her] out in a room upstairs."
Acts 9:36-37

In the Book of Acts, we find several passages describing how widows were regarded and treated in the early Church. This book gives us images both of the care of widows and also of an emerging group of widows in ministry. Some passages in Scripture and accounts of the early Church give the impression of an ecclesial order of widows, but the actual status of the widows is a matter of scholarly dispute. Mention of widows in Acts 9 is sometimes interpreted as implying the existence of an "order" of widows selected from among the larger group for ministry.

In Acts 6:1-7 we read of an emerging controversy concerning Hebrew and Hellenistic (Greek) widows. At that time, Jewish widows who had less than a week's supply of food could apply for food collected from alms at the temple. However, these widows were cut off when they became Christians. The apostles made provision for these women, but were soon being forced to mediate quarrels between the Jewish and Greek widows, the latter contended that their needs were being disregarded. Finally, the apostles appointed deacons to attend to the needs of these women, so the apostles could devote their time to prayer and preaching the Gospel.

One widow story in Scripture that delights me is the raising of Tabitha (or Dorcas, meaning "gazelle") from the dead (see Acts 9:36-42). She was such a vital part of the Christian community in Joppa that they couldn't do without her! She was full of good works and acts of charity.

When she fell sick and died, they washed her and laid her in an upper room. Since the Apostle Peter was at Lydda, which was near Joppa, the disciples sent two men to find the apostle and return with him.

Peter rose and went with them, and they took him to the upper room where the mourners had gathered. All the widows stood beside Peter, weeping and showing him the coats and garments Dorcas had made while she was with them.

So Peter sent them all outside. He knelt down and prayed, then turned to the body and said, "Tabitha, rise." She opened her eyes, and when she saw Peter she sat up. And he gave her his hand, then called the saints and widows and presented her alive. And Scripture tells us, "It became known throughout Joppa, and many believed in the Lord" (Acts 9:42).

❦ FOR REFLECTION AND DISCUSSION ❦

What does the story of Dorcas teach us about the benefits of service to God and His Church for those whose family is distant … or non-existent?

_____

_____

_____

_____

_____

_____

_____

This story shows that widows were quite active among the disciples; moreover, that they were close to each other, and also that they were much valued by the male disciples. How do you think widows are regarded in your church community?

_____

_____

_____

_____

_____

_____

_____

While we widows often do have special needs stemming from our new state in life, we also have special opportunities within the Body of Christ. For some, it is newfound time and energy to serve; for others, our sufferings give our prayers a special kind of intercessory power. How do see your role within the Church? How has it changed since becoming a widow, if at all?

_____

_____

_____

_____

_____

_____

_____

❦ **PRAYER OF THE DAY** ❦

Blessed Virgin,

When you were "widowed indeed" at the death of your beloved Son, you were entrusted to the care of the whole Church to the end of time. Look upon us, your daughters and fellow strugglers, and pray for us with empathetic wisdom. Help us to follow your example, and bring the love of Christ to all those we encounter. Amen.

A SECOND KIND OF GRIEF

"I will proclaim your name to my brothers,
in the midst of the assembly I will praise you" ...

And again, "I will put my trust in him"; and again,
"Behold, I and the children God has given me..." ...

Because he himself was tested through what he suffered,
he is able to help those who are being tested.
Hebrews 2:12-13, 18

After losing their husbands, many widows find themselves grieving a secondary loss: the death of the kind of life she and her husband enjoyed together. This is especially true when the husband was the primary breadwinner.

St. Elizabeth Seton and Praxedes Fernandez, for example, both spent long hours mending and sewing just to keep their children in the barest of necessities. In addition, Praxedes chose to become a servant in her mother's home rather than create a financial burden for her mother and unmarried sister. Because of the living situations in which they found themselves after their husbands' passing, these saints also had to protect their children from negative spiritual influences.

Even those whose husbands leave them financially well off may experience unanticipated pressures from family members – particularly adult children – about financial matters. Others may find themselves being "managed" or given assistance, whether or not they request it. All these things may heighten your sense of grief, the sense of not being in control of your own life. A second kind of loss – and, in some ways a loss that is equally profound.

❧ FOR PONDERING ❧

Do I need help from Christian friends in sorting out my financial problems? Should I pray more for help? Does God perhaps want me to live differently (perhaps more simply, or to relocate to another place) now?

_____

_____

_____

_____

_____

_____

_____

❧ PRAYER OF THE DAY ❧

Dear God,

It is sometimes surprising, all the difficulties that come up stemming from the state of life in which I now find myself. I don't always know how to deal with these new financial problems.

Come, Holy Spirit, to help all widows.

Jesus, Bridegroom of Widows, help us.

Mary, Exalted Widow, help us. Widow saints, help us.

St. Elizabeth Seton:
Battling Debt and Negative Spiritual Influences

*"O Mamma, how many friends God has provided for us in this
strange land, for they are our friends before they know us."*

St. Elizabeth Seton's daughter,
Recorded in a letter

The support and advice of friends has rarely been more tenderly portrayed
than in the friendship extended to Elizabeth Seton by the Filicchi family of
Italy. Unable to leave Italy for six months after the death of her husband,
Elizabeth and her eight-year-old daughter lived with these Italian family
friends and business partners of her husband.

In a letter back home, Elizabeth wrote: "[At Antonio Filicchi's house]
we received more than Friendship, — the most tender affection could not
bestow more, and to crown all his goodness to me he has taken my passage
[on a ship] who sails direct for New York...and accompanies us himself, as
business and a wish to be acquainted with our country has long made the
voyage necessary to him and now the desire of restoring his 'dear sister' to
her children and those she loves best, decides him to leave his dear little
wife and children — he says this is due to all my dear [husband's] love and
friendship for him."

Once in the United States, Antonio helped Elizabeth toward her
conversion, which took place soon after her return. Antonio, whose letters
and very occasional visits she treasured, became a brother to her. She
described him as "the friend, protector, and consoler of the widow and the
fatherless," who would receive a great reward in heaven.

As the wife of a prosperous New York businessman, Elizabeth had co-
founded a society for the relief of poor widows with small children.
Ironically, Elizabeth's husband died virtually bankrupt, leaving her with
five small children to support. Normally well-off relatives would have
taken care of them, but they were horrified by Elizabeth's reception into
the Catholic Church, and angered when two young women in the family

also converted to the faith.

The first convert, Cecilia, was threatened with exile from America; the anti-Catholic relatives resolved never to speak to Elizabeth or Cecelia again. They became even more furious when another daughter, a society belle, also became a fervent Catholic. Both young women died shortly afterward. Even though lung disease was a family problem, Elizabeth's family blamed her for the early death of the second young woman, since she died in Elizabeth's convent.

Since Elizabeth's health was poor, she was fearful of what might happen to her little ones if she died and had to leave them in the hands of her Protestant relatives. She determined to take up an occupation that would enable her to live on her own as a "lady," rather than live any longer with Protestant relatives. "They do not know what to do with me, but God does — and when his blessed time is come we shall know, and in the mean time he makes his poorest feeblest creature Strong."

Different clergymen, impressed by her character and teaching ideas, helped Elizabeth get situated in Maryland, first in Baltimore and then at Emmetsburg, where she founded the Sisters of Charity of Saint Joseph. As a consecrated woman with her own daughters to support (her sons were placed in a nearby Catholic boys' academy), she lived simply, and so was able to survive the grinding poverty. The snow used to come in through the roof onto their faces at night in one of their experimental dwellings.

Eventually her adult sons left to make their own futures. One became a seaman, another a businessman. Here she writes about the separation at a time when it might take many months for even a letter to get to its destination across the ocean:

"William, William, William … is it possible the cry of my heart don't reach yours; I carry your beloved name before the tabernacle and repeat it there as my prayer, in torrents of tears which our God alone understands.

"Childish weakness, fond partiality, you would say half pained if you could see from your present scene the agonized heart of your Mother. But its agony is not for our present separation, my beloved one, it is our long eternal years which press on it beyond all expression — to lose you here a few years of so embittered a life is but the common lot. But to love as I love

you and lose you forever … oh, unutterable anguish — a whole Eternity miserable, a whole Eternity the enemy of God, and such a God as he is to US — dreading so much our Faith is quite lost, having everything to extinguish, and nothing to nourish it."

❦ FOR PONDERING ❦

Since your spouse's death, have you found that your relationship with your children (whether adult or still at home) has changed? In what ways? Are you growing closer together … or farther apart?

_____

_____

_____

_____

_____

_____

_____

_____

_____

_____

God understands how debilitating the loss of a family member can be. Take it to Him, as did St. Elizabeth, before the Tabernacle. Offer it to Him along with your other sufferings.

The sand of our sufferings will produce a pearl of great price.

❦ PRAYER OF THE DAY ❦

Almighty Father, Creator of the Universe,
I am your poor, needy child.
I have nothing but rags and recriminations,
Can offer nothing but sighs and heartache.

You see it all. You know all.

Just as You watched Your Son stumble
Beneath the weight of that terrible Cross,
So you see me: poor, wretched,
And utterly alone.

You see it all. You know all.

Just give me grace enough for one more step.

Chapter Six

CRY OF REMEMBRANCE

Sixth Station
Veronica Wipes the Face of Jesus

Mary …

Most likely you knew this valiant disciple, and saw the imprint of your Son's face on that cloth long after His ascension.

Did you wipe the face of St. Joseph, just as we wiped the brow of our beloved husbands in their final moments? Did the image of your husband's face remain with you long after? When words can do little, gestures can do much.

All of us treasure the image of our husbands, if not on a cloth, then in photographs. Holy Mary, pray for us as we remember.

Jesus, we hope our husbands asked forgiveness for their sins before their deaths, even if we did not witness this. We believe that they are either in purgatory or heaven. The fully resurrected body will not be theirs – or ours – until the Last Judgment. Yet, as we struggle along without our husbands, we like to imagine their faces looking down on us with compassion and, often, humor.

❦ FOR PONDERING ❦

Is there someone who needs a tangible remembrance of your loved one, whose grief you could help to alleviate by sharing some mementos of your life together?

_____

_____

Which would you select and why?

_____

_____

_____

_____

_____

❦ PRAYER OF THE DAY ❦

Walk with me, Jesus ... (insert your own prayer here)

_____

_____

_____

_____

_____

_____

_____

Happy Birthday, Sweetheart ...

"Oh! how ephemeral is life!...
What do we do when this time is not employed for God alone?"
Blessed Conchita

Many widows find previously festive anniversaries especially painful. After her husband's death, Blessed Conchita describes a visit to the cemetery on her husband's birthday. "What a sad day for my heart, the heart of a wife and mother, was this day, my husband's birthday...." Conchita relates.

> *"Overcoming my feelings, I went to his tomb with my children to spend the morning there, right near his remains, praying and weeping ... I recalled at that time how Jesus wept over Lazarus ... death is something terrible.... My children's and my own tears moistened this soil ... then there passed through my imagination, in rapid flight, the years gone by and memories of them: sorrows, joys and dreams. In an instant all had vanished, like smoke at the breath of death....*

Johnnette Benkovic reflects: "I was not prepared for the wave of grief, nor the crush of emotion, that overwhelmed me during the first Easter liturgy following my husband Anthony's death. Though the date was different, liturgically it was the same day that Anthony had slipped into a coma. He died three days later – in that blessed span between Easter Sunday and Divine Mercy Sunday.

"I wept quietly but bitterly, cradled in the arms of my daughter, whose own tears soon mingled with mine. Though I didn't want to draw attention to myself, I was helpless to pull loose from the grip of sorrow that choked my heart.

"It reminded me of the first Sunday mass Anthony and I had attended at our parish church after our son Simon's funeral. At that mass, too, grief overcame me as I beheld the spot where Si's casket had been just a few days before. On that Sunday, other arms had held me as I sobbed quietly – strong, masculine arms that in themselves were reassuring and comforting. Arms that communicated love, and the empathy intrinsic to a suffering that is shared and known. Arms I knew that would support me and hold me up in every way. Husbandly arms.

"Those arms were forever gone from me in this life. And I would never be held by them again. I missed them! And how I missed the man whose arms they had been. Yes, I wept bitterly on that first Easter Sunday following Anthony's death. A day of resurrection imbued with the wood of the cross. Appropriate in some way, that Easter should be so: The paschal mystery experienced."

ॐ FOR REFLECTION AND DISCUSSION ॐ

You changed my mourning to dancing;
You took off my sackcloth and clothed me with gladness,
That my soul might sing praise to you without ceasing;
O Lord, my God, forever will I give you thanks.

Psalm 30:12-13

Some widows wait years to feel the same exhilaration David expressed in this psalm. Some are still waiting. Birthdays, holidays, holy days, special family traditions … Even the temporary absence of a family member changes the whole celebration. How much more, now that the one you love most is gone? To what extent have you experienced this?

_____

_____

_____

_____

_____

During this time, it may be tempting to ignore these celebrations … and yet, they are part of the fabric of life. Talk with your family and decide what traditions you want to keep, and which to modify or create anew.

_____

_____

_____

_____

_____

_____

_____

PSALM 4

Answer when I call, my saving God.
In my troubles, you cleared a way; show me favor; hear my prayer.

How long will you people mock my honor,
love what is worthless, chase after lies? Selah

Know that the LORD works wonders for the faithful;
the LORD hears when I call out.

Tremble and do not sin; upon your beds ponder in silence.
Offer fitting sacrifice and trust in the LORD.

Many say, "May we see better times!
LORD, show us the light of your face!" Selah

But you have given my heart more joy
than they have when grain and wine abound.

In peace I shall both lie down and sleep,
for you alone, LORD, make me secure.

❦ FOR PONDERING ❦

The nights can be difficult when you are a widow. The vast emptiness on the other side of the bed feels like a chasm. It keeps you on edge, poised on the precipice.

How have you been sleeping? Too much? Too little? Do you wake frequently during the night?

_____

_____

_____

_____

_____

_____

_____

_____

_____

"In peace I shall both lie down and sleep, for you alone, Lord, make me secure." Make this verse your midnight prayer.

༄ PRAYER OF THE DAY ༄

When I am anxious about what the new day brings,
"In peace I shall both lie down and sleep.
For you alone, Lord, make me secure."

When I am lonely, missing that warm presence beside me,
"In peace I shall both lie down and sleep.
For you alone, Lord, make me secure."

When _____ ,
(fill in your intention here).
"In peace I shall both lie down and sleep.
For you alone, Lord, make me secure."

THREE A'S OF COPING

*The tears were gone. And she was gone, not to return in this
life. It was, I imagine, a bit like the loss of an arm; the loss is
accepted, new ways of coping are invented, life goes on, but there
is an empty sleeve.... She and I had deliberately bound ourselves
to each other with a thousand sharings, not fearing a sundering
of the web because we should go together in the last long dive,
but now I lived with a thousand severed ties. Or perhaps more
accurately, a thousand unsevered ties stretching into eternity.*

Sheldon Vanauken
Under the Mercy

Alice von Hildebrand observed that the loss of a loved one is one of the
greatest of all human sufferings. There are many ways of coping with the
reality of this loss. Queen Victoria insisted that Prince Albert's clothing be
laid out each day, and that his table setting remain in the dining room!

Was God unjust to allow our beloved one to die and leave us? This
devilish thought might continue to tempt us, especially when we do
something that causes us to feel more bitterly our aloneness. To combat
these thoughts, Alice advises us, we must kneel in front of the crucifix and
contemplate the sufferings of Christ.

When we are engulfed with sorrow, we must choose between two
responses. The right response brings us closer to the God of peace; the
wrong response brings despair and resentment. Our grief can make us hard
and bitter ... or it can refine us and make us more sensitive to the sufferings
of others. For example, as a widow I found myself more compassionate to
single women.

What must we as Christian widows do to guard against bitterness, and
grow in compassion, as we grieve?

First, we must *accept* – "Thy will be done." We must remember that the
intensity of our suffering is proportionate to the love we have experienced.
Think: Would it have been better not to have loved so much? No, of course
not. And so, we must accept that God will heal our wounds . . . in time.

We must *acknowledge* that the good times we remember – as well as other past experiences – are real. They really happened, and are truly part of us. Let them trigger gratitude, warm your heart, and fill you with joy.

We must *anticipate* the joy we will experience when we are reunited with our husband one day. Even now, from heaven, your husband loves you even more than when he was physically present to you. You may still feel the pain of no longer feeling needed – this is natural. But we can offer our sufferings on behalf of the souls of our loved ones in purgatory. What more could we want for our beloved, than that he be united to Christ?

In our suffering, we must not allow ourselves to think, "Why did this happen to me?" or to imagine, "No one else has suffered as I suffer." Even Mary had to accept the suffering of losing such a holy husband, Joseph. He was the only one who truly understood God's gift to them, Jesus. By her example, we realize that a weeping heart can water many souls with love, and that a cross of sorrow either crushes or carries us. We must be patient with ourselves, leaning heavily on the graces God provides.

🍂 FOR PONDERING 🍂

A variety of feelings well up inside of us as we grieve. The first step is acknowledging our feelings. What emotional feelings are you feeling now?

_____

_____

_____

_____

_____

_____

While anger is a normal part of the grieving process, we must either release it or remain "stuck" in our grief. To what extent have you been angry with God for allowing your husband to die? Have you been angry with your husband for dying?

_____

_____

_____

_____

_____

_____

_____

_____

🐦 PRAYER OF THE DAY 🐦

Dear Jesus,

You know of the loneliness that we widows usually experience after the death of our spouses. You want to stand in, but also to show us who are those who can help us the most at this time.

Come, Holy Spirit show us the way.

Mary, Exalted Widow help us; widow saints help us.

St. Jane de Chantal: Longing

"I'm going ... Jesus! Jesus! Jesus!"
Final words of St. Jane de Chantal

As Jane grew older and saw her loved ones and companions pass away, she wrote, "Take my word for it — old age is miserable. My best friends have gone on to heaven and left me here on earth with all my sufferings; they were the good fruit, ready to be picked and placed on the King's banquet table, but I had to be left hanging on the vine because I was either too green or maybe rotten and full of worms."

A month before Jane died, she experienced great peace by making a final examination of her whole life to a holy archbishop. She was happy to die, then, exactly when it pleased him.

On the day of her death, Saint Vincent de Paul saw a ball of fire rising from the earth and joining itself to a large circle, which was believed to be the soul of Saint Francis de Sales.

❧ FOR PONDERING ❧

"Only the good die young" is another way of expressing these words of St. Jane. Indeed, oftentimes our loved ones are taken from us sooner than we'd expected (or wanted), leaving us with nothing but memories ... and hope.

It is worth noting here that, even though the Church has declared her a saint, St. Jane de Chantal experienced the entire range of human emotion. God does not judge us harshly for our feelings. For this reason, we can go before God with confidence, offering to Him even the parts of us we would rather not admit to another living soul.

What parts of yourself are you willing to admit to God today?

_____

_____

_____

_____

_____

_____

❦ PRAYER OF THE DAY ❦

Jesus,
> I remember …
> I celebrate …
> I believe ….

_____

_____

_____

_____

_____

_____

_____

[Personalize this prayer as you see fit.]

Chapter Seven

CRY FOR MERCY

Seventh Station
Jesus Falls the Second Time

Mary, refuge of sinners …

More than any other witness, you understood how the cross of Jesus was part of the Father's plan of salvation.

As your Son fell again, did you think of us sinners, through the centuries, coming to repentance? In your great distress, did your heart rejoice to see us repenting as we prayed these very stations?

During our long widowhood we have ample time to remember how often we fell from grace, when our own faults and sins hurt our spouses.

Mother Mary, pray for us your daughters, as we look to God for mercy.

Jesus, give us courage to confess the major sins of our married lives in the sacrament of reconciliation. You want us to have peace. Help us to believe that, in eternity, our husbands have repented of their sins against us. They do not judge us harshly now, for they are participating in the compassionate love of Your Sacred Heart for themselves and for us.

☙ FOR PONDERING ☙

Are there any resentments in me that need to be "wiped away" in the Sacrament of Reconciliation? What are they?

_____

_____

_____

_____

_____

_____

_____

☙ PRAYER OF THE DAY ☙

Walk with me, Jesus ... (insert your own prayer here)

_____

_____

_____

_____

_____

_____

_____

St. Faustina Kowalska:
When Life is Struggle

Jesus said to Sister Faustina,

"Encourage souls to place great trust in My fathomless mercy. Let the weak, sinful soul have no fear to approach Me, for even if it had more sins than there are grains of sand in the world, all would be drowned in the unmeasurable depths of My mercy"

(Diary, 55-56).

St. Faustina Kowalska (1905-1938) led a life of simplicity and deep devotion. Years after her untimely death to tuberculosis at the age of 33, her writings bore rich fruit in the Divine Mercy devotion. In the following passage of her famous *Diary,* we read of her constant struggle with empathy:

"When one is ill and weak, one must constantly make efforts to measure up to what others are doing as a matter of course. But even those matter-of-course things cannot always be managed. Nevertheless, thank You, Jesus, for everything, because it is not the greatness of the works, but the greatness of the effort, that will be rewarded. What is done out of love is not small, O my Jesus, for Your eyes see everything.

"I do not know why I feel so terribly unwell in the morning; I have to muster all my strength to get out of bed, sometimes even to the point of heroism. The thought of Holy Communion gives me back a little more strength. And so, the day starts with a struggle and ends with a struggle. When I go to take my rest, I feel like a soldier returning from the battlefield. You alone, my Lord and Master, know what this day has contained."

Diary 1310

☙ FOR REFLECTION AND DISCUSSION ☙

"… the day starts with a struggle and ends with a struggle. When I go to take my rest, I feel like a soldier returning from the battlefield." Even this cloistered nun felt this way at times. Learning to get along without a spouse is a different kind of battle – one that extends to the night as well as the day. What have been some of the most difficult times for you? What are you learning from these experiences?

_____

_____

_____

_____

_____

"It is not the greatness of the works, but the greatness of the effort that will be rewarded." How does this passage speak to you?

_____

_____

_____

_____

_____

☙ PRAYER OF THE DAY ☙

Jesus,

I trust in Your fathomless Mercy, which is new every morning.
Great is Your faithfulness to me!

St. Catherine of Genoa: Sanctifying Love

"… you will grant your pure love,
which will extinguish all other loves in me…"
Catherine of Genoa

Saint Catherine of Genoa was born to a wealthy, powerful family. As a young girl she was devoted to the Passion of Christ, and tried to enter a convent – but was refused because of her age – at thirteen. For political reasons, she was married at sixteen to Giuliano Adorni, a man of strange and dissolute ways for whom she felt only repugnance, and who squandered her fortune as well as his own. She felt abandoned by her husband and was lonely, melancholy, and unloved. She was incarcerated in her home most of the day, except for going to Mass.

The young, attractive woman sought distraction from her despair in the enjoyment of worldly vanities, but after five years of this Catherine had an overwhelming religious experience. Catherine's sister, a nun, persuaded her to go to confession. When she knelt down before the saintly priest, her heart was pierced by such tremendous love of God that she almost fainted. She was so purified by this instance of grace that she decided to spurn all worldliness and sin.

At home, Catherine went to a private room and, overwhelmed by the love of God for her, sighed deeply for her sins. She had an inner vision of Christ on the cross dripping with blood. At that time she became a daily communicant, which was very rare in those times. She suffered terribly if she thought she might be deprived of this food for her soul.

For three years Catherine did penance and ministered to the poor and sick, and continued to receive ecstatic mystical experiences. Remarkably, her husband became reconciled with her and agreed to live like brother and sister. They moved to a house in the poor district of town and devoted themselves to the care of the sick.

When Catherine was fifty years old, her husband died of a long and painful illness, thankfully at peace with God. She lived for about fifteen years after his death.

❦ FOR REFLECTION AND DISCUSSION ❦

Why do you think that the sacrament of reconciliation had such a transforming effect upon Catherine's life?

_____

_____

_____

_____

_____

It took three years of her penitence and ministry for Catherine's husband to repent of his own sinful actions and be reconciled to her. And yet, the true miracle was that the reconciliation took place at all. Why do you suppose her witness had such a transforming effect upon him?

_____

_____

_____

_____

Even though your spouse is now deceased, how can your love continue to be spiritually beneficial for him?

_____

_____

_____

_____

Psalm 34:4-11

Magnify the LORD with me;
let us exalt his name together.

I sought the LORD, who answered me,
delivered me from all my fears.

Look to God that you may be radiant with joy
and your faces may not blush for shame.

In my misfortune I called,
the LORD heard and saved me from all distress.

The angel of the LORD, who encamps with them,
delivers all who fear God.

Learn to savor how good the LORD is;
happy are those who take refuge in him.

Fear the LORD, you holy ones;
nothing is lacking to those who fear him.

The powerful grow poor and hungry,
but those who seek the LORD lack no good thing.

❧ FOR PONDERING ❧

"… nothing is lacking to those who fear him."

The Book of Proverbs reminds us: "The fear of the Lord is the beginning of wisdom." It is this wisdom that enables us to find contentment even in trying circumstances. When the psalmist said, "… nothing is lacking," he did not mean that God will always make our way easy, or our possessions multiply. Rather, the more we desire the Lord, the more our other desires begin to wane.

How has this truth taken form and shape in your life and in your loss?

_____

_____

_____

_____

_____

_____

_____

❧ PRAYER OF THE DAY ❧

Let nothing trouble you, let nothing frighten you
All things pass away, but God never changes.
Patience obtains all things.
Who possesses God wants for nothing.
God alone suffices.
St. Teresa of Avila

St. Jane de Chantal
Dryness and Desolation

"I am attacked by each and every one of the temptations my spiritual daughters tell me about; God tells me what to say to them to console them, and then there I am, stuck with all those temptations and unable to help myself."

St. Jane de Chantal

It is fascinating to contrast two different oil paintings of our saint.[1] In one she is recently widowed and in fancy dress. She looks miserable. The other one has Jane in her religious habit. She looks radiant, her eyes sparkling with joy.

Yet it is clear from her own writings and the letters of direction from Saint Francis de Sales that, for most of her life as a nun, she suffered from terrible spiritual dryness (a state in which one experiences a lack of feeling the love of Christ). Valiantly she responded to this, saying: "I never stop hoping in God, though he kill me, though he grind me into the dust of eternity."

In spite of Jane's spiritual trials, she was so revered for her love of God and neighbor that it became necessary on her visits to her different convents to stand with her back pressed closely to the wall when she was speaking, for her devotees used to try to get behind her to snip off pieces of her habit for relics!

Before Jane died, she urged the Visitation Sisters "to be in perfect unity with one another...[to) live together in all simplicity and preserve the integrity of perfect observance of the Rule."

---

[1] For a couple of online examples, go to http://www.visitationmonastery.org/stlouis/Jane.htm and http://magnificat.ca/cal/engl/08-21.htm.

❦ FOR PONDERING ❦

How does God reveal His mercy to us during times when we do not receive the spiritual consolations associated with a close relationship with God? St. Jane experienced this spiritual dryness … and the Church proclaimed her a saint!

What does this say to us, when God seems far away?

_____

_____

_____

_____

_____

_____

_____

❦ PRAYER OF THE DAY ❦

Sacred Heart of Jesus, hide me.
Immaculate Heart of Mary, cover me.
In the depths of Your mercy, bury me.
To the heights of Your Passion, lift me.
When my heart is cold and hard, soften me.
Till You take me to Your side, abide with me.

Chapter Eight

CRY OF COMPASSION

Eighth Station
The Women Console Jesus

Mary …

Were the women who braved the jeering crowd to console Jesus on the way of the cross, the same women who surrounded you when Joseph died? Surely they would not have left the mother of Love alone in her hour of need!

When we first became widows, more seasoned widows came forward to comfort and inspire us with their survival skills and their trust in you and in Jesus.

Holy Mary, pray for us with the compassion of your mother's heart.

Jesus, deep is the consolation You wish to pour into our frazzled and forlorn widowed hearts. You would have us know that we are never, never, never, alone. But we need much grace to stretch ourselves beyond our senses to know You now in an even more intimate spiritual way than before. Only You can settle us down in the peace that comes with Your presence.

❦ FOR PONDERING ❦

Where do I experience most profoundly the compassion of Christ in my life?

_____

_____

_____

_____

_____

❦ PRAYER OF THE DAY ❦

Walk with me, Jesus ... (insert your own prayer here)

_____

_____

_____

_____

_____

_____

_____

_____

St. Jane de Chantal:
When a Child Loses a Spouse

In a letter to her widowed daughter, St. Jane de Chantal advises:

My greatest wish is that you love like a true Christian widow, unpretentious in your dress and actions and especially reserved in your relationships, having nothing to do with vain, worldly young men. Otherwise, dear – even though I am very sure that your conduct is above reproach — others could question and criticize it....

I know very well, darling, of course, that we can't live in the world without enjoying some of its pleasures, but take my words for it, dearest, you won't find any really lasting joys except in God, in living virtuously, raising your children well.... If you seek happiness elsewhere, you will experience much anguish, as I well know....

I am not against the legitimate pleasure you can derive, by way of diversion, from healthy relationships with good people... Check your inclinations and surrender them to God for His glory dwelling in you, for the respect and love you owe to the memory of your beloved husband, the preservation of your good name, and the benefit of your daughter who, undoubtedly, will model herself after you.

There follows advice on how to live a Christian life in the world with Morning Prayer, commitment to do good and to avoid evil, prayers to the Holy Spirit and the Blessed Virgin, and the like. She suggests daily Mass as much as possible, readings especially from the books of Saint Francis de Sales, and a regular examination of conscience.

❦ FOR REFLECTION AND DISCUSSION ❦

Have there been particularly helpful or insightful suggestions that other widows have given you, which you want to remember in case you need to pass them on?

_____

_____

_____

_____

_____

_____

Of what benefit is a regular examination of conscience to a grieving heart?

_____

_____

_____

_____

_____

_____

❦ PRAYER OF THE DAY ❦

Blessed Mother,

After the death of your beloved spouse, Joseph, you may have longed for companionship … and yet we know you did not make sinful choices. Pray for me, that I might exercise prudence in my relationships with others, that I would not be deterred from walking in the way God has set for me.

PSALM 23

The LORD is my shepherd; there is nothing I lack.

In green pastures you let me graze;
to safe waters you lead me;
you restore my strength.

You guide me along the right path for the sake of your name.

Even when I walk through a dark valley,
I fear no harm for you are at my side;
your rod and staff give me courage.

You set a table before me as my enemies watch;
You anoint my head with oil; my cup overflows.

Only goodness and love will pursue me all the days of my life;
I will dwell in the house of the LORD for years to come.

❦ FOR REFLECTION AND DISCUSSION ❦

This is a passage that is frequently read at funerals; perhaps you even requested it at the funeral of your spouse. Was there a line that was particularly meaningful to you that day?

_____

_____

_____

_____

_____

_____

"Even when I walk through a dark valley ... you are at my side." How have you experienced this in your own life?

_____

_____

_____

_____

_____

_____

_____

_____

ॐ PRAYER OF THE DAY ॐ

Lord,

Thank You for the green pastures and safe waters that surround me. As I walk "through the valley of the shadow," help me sense the reassuring presence of my Shepherd.

Widows: Temptations and Callings

"… she who is self-indulgent is dead even while she lives."
1 Timothy 5:6

In 1 Timothy 5:3-16 we find some of the most puzzling and challenging teachings.

Honor widows who are real widows. If a widow has children or grandchildren, let them first learn their religious duty to their own family and make some return to their parents; for this is acceptable in the sight of God.

She who is a real widow, and is left all alone, has set her hope on God and continues in supplications and prayers night and day; whereas she who is self-indulgent is dead even while she lives.

Command this, so that they may be without reproach. If anyone does not provide for his relatives, and especially for his own family, he has disowned the faith and is worse than an unbeliever.

Let a widow be enrolled if she is not less than sixty years of age, having been the wife of one husband; and she must be well attested for her good deeds, as one who has brought up children, shown hospitality, washed the feet of the saints, relieved the afflicted, and devoted herself to doing good in every way.

But refuse to enroll younger widows; for when they grow wanton against Christ they desire to marry, and so they incur condemnation for having violated their first pledge. Besides that, they learn to be idlers, gadding about from house to house, and not only idlers but gossips and busybodies, saying what they should not.

So I would have younger widows marry, bear children, rule their households, and give the enemy no occasion to revile us. For some have already strayed after Satan.

If any believing woman has relatives who are widows, let her assist them; let the church not be burdened, so that it may assist those who are real widows.

I must admit that the truth of certain ideas in this famous passage never hit me until becoming a widow myself. Now I understand what a temptation gossip and idleness can be for a woman who no longer has the settled lifestyle of marriage and family. Deprived of the company of family members, we can easily develop a gossipy tongue as we go about from house to house, seeking warmth and comfort.

❦ FOR REFLECTION AND DISCUSSION ❦

Nearly every circumstance of life provides an opportunity for virtue or for vice. Loneliness can draw us more deeply into prayer or service … or reduce us to gossip or form unhealthy attachments.

What does this passage reveal about the importance of family in cultivating a balanced life in widowhood?

_____

_____

_____

_____

_____

What else can we learn about the life of a widow from this passage? Is there anything that speaks to your particular situation?

_____

_____

_____

_____

_____

When Fantasy Turns to Reality

"The virtue of the upright saves them,
But the faithless are caught in their own intrigue."
Proverbs 11:6

The fantasies I nourished throughout my married life had to do with two areas: holiness and second husbands! For years it was my conviction that my husband, Martin, was an obstacle to my holiness. Even though he had converted to the Catholic faith, as I had, his idea was that religion could be a most important part of life, but not the be-all and end-all. I, on the other hand, despite my terrible faults, had always been convinced that all Christians were called to be as holy as saints.

In my daydreams, Martin's death would mean that I no longer had to compromise with his somewhat luxurious ideas about lifestyle, including the purchase of myriad gadgets and the enjoyment of cruises and similar activities. Once I was free to make my own decisions, I would become a true daughter of Saint Francis of Assisi. Whereas my husband insisted that all the goods of the earth were provided by God to bring him joy, I couldn't wait to get rid of all the expensive items in the house, lavished upon the poor from my bountiful hands. Then I would be free to live in utter simplicity, without a car, walking everywhere, going to jail for Operation Rescue if I wished, and, of course, with a prayer life as focused as that of Saint Teresa of Avila.

Another source of fantasy involved remarriage. I imagined that bachelor friends of the family would not waste an hour after the funeral to profess their undying love, sweeping me off my feet into a glorious engagement and perfect marriage.

In my daydreams, the faults of my bachelor friends instantly disappeared because of the influence of my saintly companionship. At times of sadness or boredom, I would embroider these fantasies, planning every detail of conversation and future.

Not one to waste time, I indeed started to try to turn fantasy into reality immediately after my husband's sudden death. Sometimes the results were funny; other times humiliating. In any case, the reality – my actual feelings at the time of Martin's death – was quite different from what I had imagined beforehand.

ও FOR PONDERING ও

Whether or not you were happily married, there were probably times when you wondered what your life might have been like if you had never married (or married someone other than your husband).

If you had favorite daydreams about single life, have any of them come true? Do they continue to have the same hold on you, now that you are on your own?

ও PRAYER OF THE DAY ও

Father God,

Set a watch of angels before my mouth, and another by my heart, to weed out unworthy thoughts before they can take root and grow.

HOLY AMBIVALENCE

"I know indeed how to live in humble circumstances;
I know also how to live with abundance."
Philippians 4:12

As Alice Von Hildebrand explains in *By Grief Refined,* her beautiful book about widowhood, when a marriage is the consummation of a spousal love in Christ, focused on the unique preciousness of the beloved, there is a natural repugnance to the idea of remarriage.

On the other hand, in many marriages entered into for love, there may still be an imperfect union of hearts for many reasons. In those cases, the possibility of remarriage may seem desirable. Then again, there can be reasons for seeking remarriage that involve the legitimate needs of the children. (One of the most famous cases is that of St. Thomas More, who became a widower and re-married a woman who was devoted to his children.)

In the case of the widow-saints, the motives for their first marriages were varied. In the past, marriages were arranged with only a minimal assent on the part of the young women to be espoused. Often the desire to be a consecrated woman was thwarted by parental insistence on marriage, often for economic reasons (or political ones, in the case of royalty).

The story of St. Jane de Chantal includes many of the elements so far described. There is no doubt whatsoever that Jane loved her husband deeply. Shortly after his death, she made a private vow of consecration. Nonetheless, in spite of her desire for holiness, she fought with temptations to remarry. When we find out her circumstances, it is easy to understand why she wavered.

In those days in France, apparently an upper-class widow in Jane's legal situation would lose the right to all her husband's goods. Her children would also be disinherited, unless she moved into the house of someone in her husband's family.

Jane's father-in-law, who was eager to make use of her great talents for household management, insisted that she come to live in his manor house even though he was keeping a mistress and the domain included offspring of this liaison.

Since some of her children were still young, Jane could not enter the convent for many years. The only way she could escape from her father-in-law's house was by remarriage to one of the wealthy suitors who were seeking her hand.

During one of the first times that Francis de Sales met Jane at a social gathering, he chided her mildly for still wearing a garb that suggested she was open to remarriage, even though she had told him about her private vow. St. Jane's ambivalence may comfort widow-readers who may go through any number of years uncertain not only about availability of possible second husbands, but also about their own deepest wishes.

❦ FOR PONDERING ❦

Have you considered (or would you consider) remarriage? If your husband were talking with you today, what do you think he would say to you about your getting remarried?

What do you sense *God* is saying to you? Write about it here.

_____

_____

_____

_____

❦ PRAYER OF THE DAY ❦

In the book of Ecclesiastes, we read, "to everything there is a season, and a time for every purpose under heaven…" Lord, You are the Author of the seasons of my life. I will trust You, in good times and bad, to reveal the next step in Your good time. In the name of the Father, and the Son, and the Holy Spirit, Amen!

BLESSED MARGUERITE D'YOUVILLE:
A HEART FOR THE POOR

"When one finds a worthy wife, her value is far beyond pearls ...
She reaches out her hand to the poor, and extends her arms to the needy."
Proverbs 31:10, 20

Even though the women saints of the past seldom thought in precisely these terms, their stories make it clear that plunging into care for the needy provided healing of their own sadness and loneliness.

Blessed Marguerite d'Youville, an 18th century Canadian saint, was left virtually bankrupt after paying off her husband's gambling debts. She supported her family by opening a small shop and selling her needlework, cloth, and sundries. Soon the customers discovered in this gracious businesswoman and holy widow not only a source of good supplies but also an ear for their troubles.

Yet this was not enough. She began to turn her attentions toward those too poor to frequent her shop. Blessed Marguerite d'Youville received much of her formation as a helper of the poor of the city of Montreal from her spiritual director, Father Dulescoat. He saw in this widow the gifts of heart and mind necessary to develop a full-scale approach to the miseries of the needy.

In a short biography of his saintly mother, Marguerite's priest son, Charles, wrote this about her relationship to this director: "She was not one of those persons who importune their confessors from morning till night, piling up a hundred conferences without drawing any profit from them ... eager to change confessors, wanting to be directed by everyone they meet...."

After this fine priest's death, Father Normant became Marguerite's director. He was as interested in the growth of her own soul, especially through devotion to the Sacred Heart and to the Holy Family, as in the charity to the poor that overflowed from her love of God. It was this same director who eventually encouraged Marguerite to take the poor into her own home, and to found an order of women called the Grey Sisters.

❦ FOR PONDERING ❦

Make a list of all the Christian people who have helped you since you became a widow. Why not write a note to each one telling them exactly how they helped or are still helping you?

_____

_____

_____

_____

_____

_____

_____

❦ PRAYER OF THE DAY ❦

Our Lady of the Visitation,

Thank you for the help you sent me early in my widowhood; there were so many priests, mentors, and friends who are strong believers in your Son.

Jesus, Second Bridegroom of Widows, help me.

Mary, Exalted Widow help us. Widow saints, help me.

Chapter Nine

CRY OF DIMINISHMENT

Ninth Station
Jesus Falls Again

Mary …

Despite your unique and exalted privileges as Mother of God, you must have felt your status in the world fall when you were no longer "Joseph's wife" but only a poor widow.

In our times, most of us grieve our new state each time we fill out a form and are forced to check the "widow" box instead of the "married" box. Sometimes our social life falls because we are not part of a couple. Often, our income falls as well.

Mother Mary, pray for us your daughters as we feel our place in the world diminish.

Jesus, throughout Scripture, Your people were exhorted to honor needy widows. Purify the minds of all widows from negative images of widowhood. Show us if You want to provide us with second husbands. In Your new covenant, we are offered a new consecrated state, living to serve Your church. If our new vocation is to have You as our Second Bridegroom, show us how.

❦ FOR PONDERING ❦

Have I found my new status as "widow" diminishing in any way? If so, how?

_____

_____

_____

_____

_____

_____

❦ PRAYER OF THE DAY ❦

Walk with me, Jesus ... (insert your own prayer here)

_____

_____

_____

_____

_____

_____

_____

Turning the Heart Toward Jesus

"I wish I were dead, because I am afraid that if it keeps on long enough I might stumble...how I wish at those times [of darkness] that I were already in Purgatory, where the only direction you can go is up, so that I can be sure I would eventually be reunited with God forever...."

St. Elizabeth Seton

Perhaps at this stage of your reading, you are feeling something like this: "How the widow-saints dealt with their new state of life is wonderful. I admire them. But I can't be that way. Maybe for a few hours a day, but all day? Come on! Most of the time I just feel desperate or depressed, or plain confused."

The holy widows did not get to be the way they were just by willing it or wishing it. Rather, they opened themselves to Jesus as a Second Bridegroom in the depths of their hearts, so that they were able to respond fully to His leadings.

What does it mean to experience "bridal graces," especially if our prayer life is in crisis because of grief? Our Second Bridegroom delights in wooing each of us in a way that is personal as well as classic. For instance, some women of prayer find Christ in the sudden sight of a little violet by the road, because its unexpected appearance reassured them of the love of Jesus.

Another may recognize her Second Bridegroom only if the Lord appears in a vision and tells her so. Still others experience Christ's warm arms around them through the embrace of brothers and sisters in the family or Church.

The nature of these bridal graces can vary from person to person.

Elizabeth Seton would simply talk to Christ all day; she expresses her confidence in Christ as her Sacred Bridegroom primarily by her trust in His providence in all circumstances. And yet, her writings amply demonstrate that those who have decided to choose Jesus as the Second Bridegroom will not experience perpetual bliss. Here we clearly see the Second Bridegroom not as a source of joy but still as the true Savior to whom all our sufferings are to be offered as a high "bridal gift."

Writing about her time in the convent, St. Elizabeth says, "I write about God and talk of him as if I really know him, and most of the time I am sure I do know some things about him, and I do believe that there is great value in the pain and suffering I undergo every day, since I desire nothing else than this treasure of faith, hope and charity and the knowledge that I am doing everything I possibly can to find out what God wants me to do..."

So great were these interior sufferings that she could write: "I wish I were dead, because I am afraid that if it keeps on long enough I might stumble...how I wish at those times [of darkness] that I were already in Purgatory, where the only direction you can go is up, so that I can be sure I would eventually be reunited with God forever.... If I can keep from offending God in spite of all this, then I am content with whatever it may please him to allow me to suffer, even if I must suffer for the rest of my life; I want only to do it knowing that he wants me to, and that in suffering I am being faithful to him."

❦ FOR PONDERING ❦

What areas of your life do you find most difficult to be open to the Second Bridegroom right now? Tell Him about them.

_____

_____

_____

_____

_____

_____

_____

☙ PRAYER OF THE DAY ☙

I feel you walking with me, Jesus, when ... (finish your prayer here).

_____

_____

_____

_____

_____

_____

_____

_____

LOVE SONGS OF BRIDAL MYSTICISM

*"What a great thing is love, provided always that it returns to its origin;...
flowing back again to its source it acquires fresh strength
to pour itself forth once again."*
St. Bernard of Clairvaux

The dark "bridal graces" of Elizabeth Seton have an emotional tone quite different from what we find in the explicitly bridal mysticism of a Blessed Angela of Foligno.

Traditional bridal mysticism takes its themes from the Song of Solomon (or Song of Songs) of the Old Testament. It possesses a sublimated erotic nature linked to the notion of courtly love as found, for example, in the love poetry of Hadewijch (13th century):

> All things
> are too small
> to hold me,
> I am so vast
>
> In the Infinite
> I reach
> for the Uncreated
>
> I have
> touched it,
> it undoes me
> wider than wide
>
> Everything else
> is too narrow
>
> You know this well,
> you who are also there.

🐦 **PRAYER OF THE DAY** 🐦

How would you characterize your relationship with God, or your sense of Him as "Second Bridegroom," since you became a widow? How has God been like a husband to you? Write your thoughts in the form of a prayer or poem.

_____

_____

_____

_____

_____

_____

_____

_____

_____

THE SECOND BRIDEGROOM:
PROTECTOR, COMFORTER, AND LOVER

"Alleluia! The Lord has established his reign, [our] God, the almighty.
Let us rejoice and be glad and give him glory.
For the wedding day of the Lamb has come,
His bride has made herself ready.
She was allowed to wear a bright, clean linen garment."
(The linen represents the righteous deeds of the holy ones.)

Revelation 19:6-8

Yes, Jesus is the Second Bridegroom … our Protector, Comforter, and Lover. These themes appear again and again in the writings of the widow-saints. I offer them for your consideration, so that you would realize that Jesus does have the power to lift you, in a manner and time suitable to your own temperament, up to a new level of the Spirit, where your joy in Him will be complete.

Jesus Our Protector …

Saint Vincent de Paul urged Saint Louise de Marillac and the Sisters of Charity they founded together to trust only in Christ as their protector. Is not the role of protector part of the mission of the husband to the wife, and even more so the Second Bridegroom?

"Do you know what God does to a soul that is deprived of all human comfort and support?" he had asked. "... It is his pleasure to lead such a soul...and if she clings to Him with entire confidence, He will support her with His own hand and never let her sink."

During her husband's terrible illness, first aboard ship and then in quarantine, Saint Elizabeth Seton wrote her friend that during the terrible nights when he was struggling to breathe, "If I could forget my God one moment at these times I should go mad — but He hushes all — Be still and know that I am God your Father."

In the same letter about anticipating the loss of her husband she writes:

"If we do not meet again here — there we shall be separated no more — if I have lost them now, their gain is infinite and eternal. How often I tell my William, 'When you awake in that world you will find nothing could tempt you to return to this, you will see that your care over your wife and little ones, was like a hand only to hold the cup which God himself will give if he takes you.'"

Christ Our Comforter ...

After becoming a widow, Elizabeth was much consoled by the comfort to be found in faith and trust in Christ as her Second Bridegroom. In one of her first letters after the death of her husband, she confides in her reader that her life would be death without the help of God, her comforter.

"It pleased God to try me very hard in many ways — but also to bestow such favors and comforts that it would be worse than disobedience not to dwell on his Mercy while I must bow to his dispensations." She found great comfort always in the thought of the joy of eternity and turned her grief about the death of not only her husband but of other loved ones into hope and joy in the thought of the delights of heaven.

As we also need to do, our American saint flung herself at the feet of her Heavenly Spouse, seeking in him the happiness she had lost from the death of her husband: "Suffer me to remain at thy Feet. There it is that I find my happiness O Divine Jesus! — my Joy, my Delight, that Peace of God...."

The Bridegroom as Lover ...

In the foreword to *Angela of Foligno: Complete Works* we read: "The marrow of Angela's inner life [was] her passionate love affair with the suffering God-man." The Holy Spirit told this Italian widow: "I will hold you closely to me and much more closely than can be observed with the eyes of the body."

So important for a widow, who no longer has someone close to enjoy and appreciate her, is this locution Blessed Angela heard on the road from Assisi to Foligno. Jesus said: "Your whole life, your eating, drinking, sleeping, and all that you do are pleasing to me."

Here is Angela's account of the sense of intimacy that came after her return from the pilgrimage that marked an entrance into still more mystical states of union: "Once I was back home, I felt so peaceful and was so filled with divine sweetness that I find no words to express my experience; and there was also in me a desire to die." (She wanted to reach the source of this happiness and at the same time was afraid of losing it.) "I lay at home enthralled by this great consolation and in a state of languor for eight days." Angela understood that she was not only listening to Christ but feeling him within her. "You do not see me but you feel me."

Jesus called her "my temple, my delight." And said, "You are holding the ring of my love. From now on you are engaged to me and you will never leave me."

Here is how Blessed Marie of the Incarnation describes her sense of Christ the Second Bridegroom as lover: "It is impossible to say how agonizing this love is and yet the soul has no desire to free itself, except to possess him whom she loves. It seems to it that it has spiritual arms which are constantly extended to embrace him....All its sighing, all its attention, even its life are constantly in this state of predilection for its well-beloved.... I cannot explain to what the Beloved reduces the soul in order to make it pursue him all the more. He secures it by double chains. He holds it captive under his own loving laws and despoils it completely in order to make it follow him."

All this yearning prepared Marie of the Incarnation of Tours, France, for the mystical marriage with Christ that took place some eight years after she was widowed: 'Then, engulfed in the presence of this adorable Majesty, Father, Son, and Holy Spirit, adoring him in the awareness and acknowledgement of my lowliness, the Sacred Person of the Divine Word revealed to me that he was in truth the spouse of the faithful soul. I understood this truth with absolute certainty and this very understanding became the imminent preparation for this grace to be effected in me. At that moment, this adorable Person seized my soul and embracing it with indescribable love united it to himself, taking it as his spouse." She went on to say: "Hitherto [the soul] had been in continual longing and expectation.... Now the soul has no further longing because it possesses him whom it loves. The soul is all his."

❦ FOR PONDERING ❦

Have you experienced Christ as your Protector, Comforter, and Lover? Write about it.

_____

_____

_____

_____

_____

_____

_____

_____

_____

_____

_____

WIDOW SAINTS ON DIFFICULT SOLITUDE

Even though Saint Louise de Marillac (1591-1660) had no wish to remarry, her early widowhood was lonely and depressing. After her husband died she removed herself from the social frivolities of the Parisian court, and experienced intense feelings of sinfulness for not having chosen the religious life before her marriage.

Although she belonged to the upper strata of seventeenth-century Parisian society, when her husband died St. Louise had to sell their large house and move into a poorer neighborhood. She was delighted to have the freedom now to live more simply with one maid instead of a retinue and without obligations to attend functions at theaters and drawing rooms. And yet, so beloved was she by her rich friends, they often came in their luxurious carriages to visit her and benefit from her good counsel and her prayers. Of course, God had his own plan for St. Louise, who went on to found the Sisters of Charity.

By contrast, Conchita wrote in her diary that just before her husband died, with "my forehead resting on the forehead of him who was so good to me, I consecrated myself to God to be all for Him." She never wavered in this decision; yet, after her children were grown, she described the last twenty years of her life as a time of painful solitude. She died in 1937.

Saint Elizabeth Seton loved her husband dearly. Her great wish, after his death and her own conversion to the Roman Catholic faith, was to be a religious sister in some way consonant with mothering her five young children. Yet when she met an ardent Catholic man in her travels who seemed to understand her, she felt drawn to him and had to struggle to overcome the desire to remarry in the light of her higher calling. She described herself as having an "inflammable heart."

Years later Elizabeth, hearing about a widow-friend who was considering remarriage, advised that she should stay single. The reason she gave was that even in the best of marriages the adjustment of one personality to the other is so difficult that it was better to be alone!

❦ FOR REFLECTION AND DISCUSSION ❦

When have you found your solitude most difficult to bear?

_____

_____

_____

_____

If your new state has resulted in a drastic change in finances, how has this affected the friendships and other relationships that you had when you were married?

_____

_____

_____

_____

What does it mean to have an "inflammable heart"? Does it necessarily involve an inability to feel?

_____

_____

_____

_____

❦ PRAYER OF THE DAY ❦

Lord Jesus, when I struggle to keep hold of my "inflammable heart," draw me close to your Sacred Heart. Mary, mother of widows, pray for me.

LOVE PSALMS

How precious is your love, O God!
We take refuge in the shadow of your wings.

We feast on the rich food of your house;
from your delightful stream you give us drink.

For with you is the fountain of life, and in your
light we see light.

Psalm 36:8-10

❦ FOR PONDERING ❦

When do you most often experience God as "light"? How has He been your Provider?

_____

_____

_____

_____

_____

_____

_____

_____

❦ FOR REFLECTION AND DISCUSSION ❦

You have tested my heart, searched it in the night.
You have tried me by fire, but find no malice in me.

My mouth has not transgressed as humans often do.
As your lips have instructed me, I have kept the way of the law.

My steps have kept to your paths; my feet have not faltered.
I call upon you; answer me, O God. Turn your ear to me; hear my prayer.

Show your wonderful love, you who deliver with your right arm
those who seek refuge from their foes.

Keep me as the apple of your eye;
hide me in the shadow of your wings…

Psalm 17:3-8

As married women, we have known the refuge of a husband's embrace. As widows, we learn to experience this safety "under the shadow."

Write about a time you experienced these things (or wanted to) in your own life.

SHOULD I REMARRY?

"Imperfect as we are, we somehow transform into poison the very
medicine the Great Physician prescribes for our healing ... let us
surrender ourselves lovingly to the will of our heavenly Father and
cooperate with His plan to unite us intimately to Himself through
suffering. If we do that, He will become all for us: our brother, son,
husband, mother, our all in all. Courage!...I beg our Lord to help
you find the rich treasure which His Goodness has hidden at the
very core of the pain that comes to you from His hand."
St. Elizabeth Seton to her widowed daughter Francoise

It is often supposed that most holy widows were unhappily married women who longed all their lives to be consecrated, and who rushed immediately after the death of their spouses into the convent. While it is true that many of the widow-saints do fit this pattern, there are quite a number who do not. Some were very content in their marriages, and some who later became nuns, sisters, or third order celibates thought long and hard before making this choice.

Many Catholics also believe that if a widow does remarry, this is proof that she is not holy. I do not think that such a conclusion is valid. While it is sometimes part of the holiness of a consecrated woman that she has sacrificed marriage, this does not mean that marriage or remarriage need be a barrier to holiness. Since most canonization procedures in modern times have as their starting point the desire of men and women in particular orders to see their founder or foundress recognized as holy, we simply know much more about holy men and women in the consecrated life than holy laypeople.

Nonetheless, I found I could not help but be struck by how many of the widow-saints did reject even the possibility of remarriage in favor of a publicly or privately consecrated vow, following in this choice the preponderance of advice for widows to be found in Scripture. After a beautiful marriage, many women choose not to remarry. However, St. Thomas More remarried only one month after the burial of his first wife.

He was not callous – he needed a mother for his children, and a wife to manage his house.

Remarriage after the death of a spouse is not a sin. We should not judge those who do remarry – it *is* possible (rare, but possible) to have two great loves.

❦ FOR REFLECTION AND DISCUSSION ❦

Are there circumstances in your life that seem to point toward (or away from) remarriage?

_____

_____

_____

_____

_____

_____

_____

What is God teaching you through this "medicine" of widowhood ... and how does it affect your desire (or lack of desire) to seek this kind of intimacy in marriage again?

_____

_____

_____

_____

_____

_____

_____

St. Elizabeth Seton:
On Dangerous Spiritual Friendship

Trust in the LORD and do good
that you may dwell in the land and live secure.

Find your delight in the LORD
who will give you your heart's desire.

Be still before the LORD; wait for God.
Psalm 37:3-4, 7

For St. Elizabeth Seton, as for many a woman, the transition to experiencing Christ as her true love involved having to face the limited satisfaction that can be derived from human love, limitations based both on Church law and the metaphysics of finite love.

For example, the special love she had for her married friend and protector Antonio Filicchi — while returned from his side in essence — did not match hers in terms of the frequency of their correspondence. No doubt the infrequency of his letters may be attributed both to Antonio's own caution as well as his lack of time for such writings.

Struggles with feelings of neglect are a constant theme in the correspondence. That he didn't always send her a new address as he traveled about can be seen from this excerpt: "You said you would not write yet if it had been in your power you would have sent at least your direction [address]. Often my heart cries out to God for you and if I did not commit you wholly to him I should be very unhappy."

Sometimes she dealt with her disappointment with a charming humor: "Tonino, Tonino [Antonio's nickname] — how I long to meet you in your state of perfection, where I shall receive the transfusion of your affections without your exertions...."

As a spiritual friend he became a soul mate to her, and she experienced the pain of the fact that as a married man he could never be part of her daily life in the way she would have loved. This is expressed quite subtly, for she was clearly aware of the dangers of drawing him too close to her under the circumstances. He did not encourage her to write to him on his business travels too often.

In a letter to him she wrote: "I begin now wishfully to watch every evening hoping...for a letter from — this you may think childish dear Antonio but remember you have not a female heart, and mine is most truly and fondly attached to you, as you have proved when I have been most contradictory and troublesome to you — fearing too much not to possess your invaluable affection."

And then, in another plaintive letter she said that "if I was your brother, Antonio, I would never leave you for one hour — but as it is I try rather to turn every affection to God, well knowing that there alone their utmost exercise cannot be misapplied and most ardent hopes can never be disappointed."

Such sufferings of loneliness only led Elizabeth the more to realize that, for her, Jesus could be her only Bridegroom. "I should wish earnestly my most dear Brother never to think of you with tenderness but when calling on Almighty God to bless you, then often my heart overflows and exhausts the sighs and tears of affection which at all other times are not carefully repressed — and far from feeling less interest for you and less value for your affection it has never so earnestly so anxiously prayed for you as during the few weeks past in which it has been pained by your neglect...."

How lovable must this widow have been who, in this vulnerable a manner, was able to write to her happily married friend: "Dear, dear Antonio why must I speak to you in a manner so little conformed to the feelings of my heart — but you know yourself drew the line, and the kindness and sweetness of affection must be veiled — from the searcher of hearts it cannot, and it delights me to consider that he also sees its sincerity, simplicity and holiness."

Looking back we can see how the movements of what she herself called "my inflammable heart" were a preparation for her complete self-surrender to Christ in her religious vows. "Many seek to love God by different methods but there is none so short and so easy as to do everything for his love, to set this seal on all our actions, and keep ourselves in his presence by the commerce of the heart with him in full simplicity without embarrassment or disguise."

In a certain way, contrasting the flavor of this passage with that of the passionate writings of some other widow-saints, we could say that Elizabeth experienced Christ not so much as Second Bridegroom but as Second Husband, like a spouse in a long-term relationship, always near at hand.

❦ FOR REFLECTION AND DISCUSSION ❦

How would you advise a widow friend who found herself depending on a married friend in a way that could give rise to scandal or temptation?

_____

_____

_____

_____

_____

_____

How does finding "your delight in the Lord" keep all other relationships in proper perspective? Can you sincerely love God, and still be vulnerable to temptation? If so, what are some ways to guard against improper attachments?

_____

_____

_____

_____

_____

_____

_____

CHAPTER TEN

CRY OF RELINQUISHMENT

Tenth Station
Jesus Is Stripped

Mary …

Did you keep any of your Son's things after His death? Perhaps, you even kept some of Joseph's belongings? We cannot know for certain. What we do know is that Jesus was parted from his clothes by force, an act of violence.

After the death of our husbands, it was a painful process to go through their possessions. As we stripped away those clothes, we felt the memories connected to those clothes slip away as well.

In another sense we feel stripped of everything our husband's presence meant to us, especially on anniversaries, birthdays, family holidays, and religious holy days. Holy Mary, pray for your daughters as we struggle to place all our losses into the hands of God.

Jesus, You wept at the death of Lazarus – and though it is not recorded, no doubt You cried when Joseph died, too. Even so, You also told us not to grieve as unbelievers do. Grief takes many forms; some of these forms are surprising, such as mourning over an article of our husband's clothing. We beg You to turn each experience of loss into gratitude for the good times.

We hope for that day when our resurrected bodies will be clothed in unimaginable splendor, and we will be reunited with our loved ones. In the meantime, give us grace to be glad to be stripped of what we no longer need, and to help those who have less especially the starving and homeless.

❦ FOR PONDERING ❦

In what ways have you been "stripped" -- or feel as though you still need to let go?

_____

_____

_____

_____

_____

_____

❦ PRAYER OF THE DAY ❦

Walk with me, Jesus ... (insert your own prayer here)

_____

_____

_____

_____

_____

_____

_____

_____

_____

_____

_____

BLESSED ANGELA OF FOLIGNO: A HEART WITHIN GOD'S HEART

"For all of you are children of the light and children of the day. We are not of the night or of darkness. Therefore, let us not sleep as the rest do, but let us stay alert and sober…. For God did not destine us for wrath, but to gain salvation through our Lord Jesus Christ, who died for us, so that whether we are awake or asleep we may live together with him. Therefore, encourage one another and build one another up, as indeed you do."
1 Thessalonians 5:5-6, 9-11

Some widows are surprised at the intensity of their grief. This is especially true for those who, like I did, anticipated a certain ambivalence about being liberated from a wretched marital situation … or for those who saw in widowhood a way to pursue holiness unencumbered by the worldly goals of their husbands. Even so, there is often much grief.

A most startling story of ambivalence in the crisis of widowhood can be found in the words of Blessed Angela of Foligno (1248-1309), an Italian Franciscan mystic. Blessed Angela had been a sinful married woman. It is unclear if her infidelities went as far as outright adultery, but her confessor and scribe indicated that her sins were mortal, deadly to her soul. It is said she had several sons, but their lives were cut short when her immediate family died in 1288, leaving her alone.

After her conversion, but before widowhood, Angela was eager to live for Christ alone but frustrated by the worldliness of her mother, husband, and sons. She said:

"At that time my mother, who had been a great obstacle to me, died. In like manner my husband died, as did all my sons in a short space of time. Because I had already entered the aforesaid way, and had prayed to God for their death, I felt a great consolation when it happened … since God had conceded me this aforesaid favor, my heart would always be within God's heart, and God's heart always within me."

In her late thirties, Angela made a pilgrimage to Assisi, about twenty miles' distance from Foligno. Having a sudden dramatic conversion, Angela became a Third Order Franciscan. When her family died, she decided to live in poverty, penance, and care of the needy, free from the bondage of the expected social life for women of her class. Soon the holy mystic was surrounded by loving disciples, both women and men.

Angela was so theatrical in the expression of her religious emotions that even her followers didn't always know what to do with her. Her visions left her with so much fire, fervor, and joy that when she heard anyone speak of God she would cry aloud in public.

At first, after her conversion on the road to Assisi, Angela experienced tremendous consolations; but later she went through periods of demonic affliction and hideous temptations, some to sins she had never even imagined in her youth. Blessed Angela's account of her life of prayer is contained in *The Book of Divine Consolation*, which was one of the most beloved and popular writings of a woman mystic during many of the centuries following her death. Much of her writing was dictated to her confessor, Franciscan Brother Arnaldo.

ॐ FOR PONDERING ॐ

Are there any situations in your life about which you have experienced feelings of ambivalence, uncertain whether the roots of your experience were divine, demonic … or merely human? Write about it.

_____

_____

ॐ PRAYER OF THE DAY ॐ

"Let us not sleep as the rest do…" This, I can relate to! Lord, work in me through all the circumstances of my life, that I might be truly a "child of the day," a beautiful reflection of Your divine life.

Psalm 38: 6-15

I am stooped and deeply bowed; all day I go about mourning.
My loins burn with fever; my flesh is afflicted.
I am numb and utterly crushed; I wail with anguish of heart.
My Lord, my deepest yearning is before you;
*   my groaning is not hidden from you.*
My heart shudders, my strength forsakes me;
*   the very light of my eyes has failed.*
Friends and companions shun my pain; my neighbors stand far off.
Those who seek my life lay snares for me; they seek my misfortune,
*   they speak of ruin; they plot treachery all the day.*
But I am like the deaf, hearing nothing, like the dumb,
*   saying nothing,*
Like someone who does not hear, who has no answer ready.
LORD, I wait for you; O Lord, my God, answer me.

It's amazing how the rest of the world does not stop to wait for us in our grief.

The postman still arrives with the bills, as though the one who always wrote the checks still lives there.

The solicitors still call and attempt to pique our interest in an Orlando timeshare, unaware that a relaxing vacation no longer sounds as good as it used to.

The grass still grows tall, oblivious to the silence of the mower standing idly in the shed.

The friends and neighbors who urged us to call them if we need anything have gone back to earning a living and cheering at their children's ballgames.

The empty casserole dishes have been emptied, washed, and returned. Sometimes we skip dinner altogether because it's too much trouble to cook for one.

The kids have returned to their homes and families, and the deserted family pew is so wide that you are tempted to skip church altogether rather than endure Mass alone.

But you don't. You keep moving, keep doing, keep going. Because you promised you would, promised your children, your friends, your beloved husband. Because you must.

❦ PRAYER OF THE DAY ❦

Somehow the rest of the world does not stop to wait for those who are grieving.

So, Lord, I wait for you.

O Lord, my God, answer and deliver me.

Ronda's Story:
Letting Go of Adult Children

"My little children, I will be with you only a little while longer. …I give you a new commandment: love one another. As I have loved you, so you also should love one another. This is how all will know you are my disciples, if you have love for one another."
John 13:33-35

After my husband's death, I lived with my daughter and her family, then left to teach at the Franciscan University of Steubenville for a time. When I returned to my daughter's house, I was too bossy about many trivial things – such as car arrangements. It really strained our relationship.

When I left to teach at Our Lady of Corpus Christi (in Texas), and then on to other places, I saw this daughter and her family only on holidays and summers. As I began to let go of bossiness and harsh judgments, and turned my family over to God, the healing began.

The sad truth is that many mothers find it difficult to let go of their adult children and let them make their own choices. We like to feel needed, and resist their normal desire for autonomy. St. Monica, a widow, was greatly attached to her son Augustine. Before his conversion, when he left from Africa to Italy she insisted on going with him. But he didn't want her to accompany him, so to escape he sailed on a boat the night before. She followed him anyhow.

❦ FOR PONDERING ❦

Like St. Monica, are you sometimes too possessive of your adult children? How do you bring your anxieties about your adult children to Jesus in prayer? Do you really trust that He loves them and will bring good out of every mistake they make?

_____

_____

_____

_____

_____

_____

_____

❦ PRAYER OF THE DAY ❦

Lord of our lives, You know that some wives become widows when they still have small or teen-age children. It is hard for them. Even when our children are older, we often miss the advice our husbands would have given us about how to deal with their problems, especially how much to intervene in financial needs of adult children. Teach us also how to be the best grandmothers possible, if we are blessed with grandchildren.

Jesus, Bridegroom of widows, help us.
Mary, Exalted Widow, help us.
Widow saints, help us.

Blessed Conchita:
Widowed Mother

"In my life as a child, my family life had so many imperfections! ... Let us see whether as a widow, I am going to seek my perfection and become a saint in carrying out the sacred duties of a mother."

Blessed Conchita

Conchita, the holy Mexican woman, co-founded several orders. Nonetheless, she always thought her duties as a mother were her primary concern. The widow's concern to raise her children to be holy occupied the greatest part of her time. Conchita prayed separately for each one regarding what was necessary in terms of virtues and state of life.

She felt unutterable anguish when one of her boys died while her husband was still alive, and then again, when the youngest of the eight living ones suddenly drowned in the swimming pool of the house. Another son died at age eighteen after a sickness, probably typhoid fever.

Two of Conchita's children took religious vows — her son Manuel as a Jesuit missionary, entailing the terrible prospect of lifelong separation, and her daughter Concha as a contemplative Sister of the Cross. She had to watch this daughter die also, this one of tuberculosis. The four surviving children became exemplary laypersons.

Conchita's biographer, Philipon, interviewed her four adult children, who all said she was a wonderful mother. She was always pleasant, full of fun, spontaneous, loving, firm and energetic, and normal, never putting on holy affectations, visiting with guests of all kinds, and always helping the poor. The only fault her children could mention was a fondness for candy.

Conchita prayed for detachment from earthly things, yet she did not think it necessary to pretend to be so detached as to feel no pain at the gradual loss of her family. After her last son's marriage, Conchita wrote in a manner that will endear her to many a mother-widow:

Now all is over for me. God gave me nine children. He has taken away all nine, may He be blessed! Two religious, the others dead or married. All, one after another, have been snatched from my maternal heart. Their beds, including that of my husband, are now empty and here I am now alone. Yet no, not alone, I have Christ who does not die, who does not part from me, and who will never abandon me.

❧ FOR PONDERING ❧

"Here I am now alone. Yet no, not alone, I have Christ... who will never abandon me." Does this resonate within your heart? When do you feel Christ closest to you?

_____

_____

_____

_____

_____

❧ PRAYER OF THE DAY ❧

Blessed Mother Mary,

After the deaths of your husband and your Son, no doubt there were times when your solitude was more than you felt you could bear. Pray for me, that in my solitude I would become not bitter, but thankful.

St. Brigid of Sweden:
Entrusting A Child to God

"Train up a child in the way he should go,
and when he is old he shall not depart from it."
Proverbs 22:6

Saint Brigid of Sweden, who died in 1373, was the mother of eight. One daughter, Ingeborg, became a nun early in her life. Another, Cecilia, was a nun but left the convent to marry. Even in our times such a change of mind could cause a mother dismay; how much more so in her times!

In Jorgensen's famous biography, Christ tells Brigid that this daughter, Cecilia, belonged to him, and that he chose that she would better grow as a married woman, so the mother should not mourn.

We find that Brigid's daughter Cecilia was twice married and widowed. At the end of her life, she lived as a widow in the monastery founded by her mother, Brigid, where one of Cecilia's own daughters was a nun.

Brigid had problems with another daughter, Karin, as well. When she was twenty years old, Karin was with her mother in Rome but not allowed to go about, since she was too attractive. She had to stay in her room while the others in the group went around visiting churches. The young woman, in despair, thought about using a poisonous ointment to mar her face just so she could get out of the house.

Brigid and her confessor forbade this strategy, and told Karin that God would protect her from shame and dishonor. She decided to go off alone to disfigure herself, but just as she started to do this, a big rock fell on her head, which injured her without killing her.

Brigid then put her daughter under the guidance of her confessor, Master Petrus. As a result of his holy advice, Karin placed herself in the hands of Saint Sebastian, and she felt brave enough to venture outside the confines of her home. Once at a pilgrim inn some bandits threatened to rape, but God sent angels disguised as soldiers to protect her.

❦ FOR PONDERING ❦

Are you ever afraid for your children? Is there any choice your child could make that you would find difficult to entrust the outcome into God's hands? Anything your child could do that you feel incapable of handling, now that you are alone?

_____

_____

_____

_____

_____

_____

It's important to bear in mind two important truths:

1. You are never truly alone. Even now, you are surrounded by the hosts of heaven.
2. Your child belongs to God, a heavenly Father who is intimately concerned for your child's welfare, and loves your child even more than you do.

❦ PRAYER OF THE DAY ❦

Heavenly Father, into Your hands I commit my child(ren)'s spirit(s). Replace my dread with hope, that I might unclench my fists and hold them up for You to fill.

Chapter Eleven

CRY OF PAIN

Eleventh Station
Jesus Is Nailed to the Cross

Mary …

You had to watch your Son endure one of the worst deaths ever devised. You saw the nails, blood, wounds, and his horrible, agonizing pain. At the crucifixion, you reflected the pain and strain your Son was experiencing. You became a mirror of His crucifixion.

Many widows recall having witnessed the awful, gut-wrenching miseries of a husband's suffering. Like you, Mary, we became mirrors of that suffering. Our faces, previously more often expressive of lighthearted joy, now manifest the heavy sadness of death.

Jesus, through our baptism each of us is incorporated into the paschal mystery. This means that, like You, we will all experience the passion, death and resurrection. Seen in this light, the loss of our husbands unites us to You in a profound way. Your mother shows us how to endure our cross and how to unite it to Yours. Help us to use our suffering and grief as a conduit of redemptive love that can lead others to You. Mary, our Mother, pray for us now and at the hour of death.

❧ FOR PONDERING ❧

Our countenance often reflects the emotions of our heart. What do you think people "see" when they look at you? Whose faces have you found especially "beautiful" in this your time of grief? What did they reflect?

_____

_____

_____

_____

_____

_____

❧ PRAYER OF THE DAY ❧

Walk with me, Jesus ... (insert your own prayer here)

_____

_____

_____

_____

_____

_____

_____

MARY, EXALTED WIDOW

*"There remains for you to pass the last stage of your life
imitating My Mother for obtaining graces for the Works of the
Cross.... Carry on your mission, imitate the virtues of Mary in
her solitude, virtues which brought about her union with Me,
her obedience to My will and her desire of heaven."*

Jesus to Blessed Conchita

In a certain way it seems odd to think of Mary, the Mother of the Infant
Jesus, as also His Bride, but indeed we know that it is so. Who could have
a more intimate relationship to Christ, the Second Bridegroom, than the
woman whose heart was unscarred by sin, and whose whole earthly life was
spent in union with Him?

Mary was a widow. Though she never experienced physical union
with St. Joseph, their marriage must have been sublime in terms of the
union of hearts. How Mary must have grieved to be deprived of the
daily companionship of the one man, apart from Jesus himself, who fully
understood about her Immaculate Conception and the miraculous birth
and destiny of their Son!

First as Joseph's widow, then as a bereaved mother, the story of Mary's
life includes features characteristic of each of the paths of our widowed
saints.

No doubt she exercised her motherly ministry to the needy of the
Church family, and for all those suffering.

Surely she was a penitent, offering her own pain not for her own sins
but for redemptive graces to pour down upon the Church.

She must have had the soul of a nun, her heart an enclosed garden in
her mystical communion with Christ.

Surely she came up against all the evils in the early Church with a
fearless prophetic spirit.

And as mediatrix of all graces, she served as foundress of the community
we call the Church.

I also think of Mary from heaven as exercising a widow-to-widow ministry with our saintly widows! Blessed Angela claims that the Virgin Mary obtained for her the grace of conversion from her relatively tepid state before that moment of ecstasy. Saint Louise de Marillac urged the Sisters of Charity "to take the Blessed Virgin as your only Mother."

Elizabeth Seton, before her conversion, realized that Mary could not help loving and pitying the poor souls her Son died for. She wrote: "I felt really I had a Mother which you know my foolish heart so often laments to have lost in early days — from the first remembrance of infancy I have looked in all the plays of childhood and wildness of youth to the clouds for my Mother, and at that moment it seemed as if I had found more than her...so I cried myself to sleep on her heart."

I do not think that it is an accident that so many widows find themselves in church each day after Mass praying the mysteries of the Rosary, so full of pain, but also of joy and glory. For the joy and glory of a widow is in the hope that she will one day experience the mysteries of her faith fulfilled in an eternity of happiness.

❦ PRAYER OF THE DAY ❦

After I became a widow, someone gave me a card with a picture of Mary accompanied by the following words:

Maria Excelsa Vidua
(Mary, Exalted Widow, Pray for us.)

Mary, conceived without original sin,
pray...for the gift of spiritual peace....
You whose heart was pierced by a sword,
as prophesied by Simon at the presentation of Jesus in the Temple,
to whom was prophesied by the widow Anna,
who suffered the death of your holy spouse, Joseph,
you who stood at the foot of the cross,
contemplating the death of your Son for sinners,
and accepted the plan of the Father,

I pray that you would intercede for me,
that with your example of supreme faith,
I would accept the will of the Lord,
in the hope of receiving the grace to be reunited
with everyone in His holy kingdom. Amen.

St. Jane de Chantal: Children and the Consecrated Life

Saint Jane de Chantal was not able to take steps toward becoming a consecrated nun until she had settled her children successfully. One daughter died young, while another married a brother of Saint Francis de Sales; the couple resided close to the convent Jane eventually founded.

The last of her children to be provided for was a fifteen-year-old son. For a year before the break he had been lovingly informed of his good future within the extended family. Nonetheless, in a dramatic teenage gesture he threw himself over the threshold when his mother was on her way to the convent, so everyone could see how "you trampled on your own child."

In a letter of spiritual direction, Saint Francis de Sales urged Jane de Chantal to try to plant in the soul of her son a desire to serve God: "... You will have to minimize the idea of purely human glory, but do this very gradually; as he grows up, with God's help, we shall think of specific ways of doing this."

✿ FOR PONDERING ✿

Children express their grief and loss in different ways at various stages of development. Young children may not immediately grasp the meaning of a significant loss – such as the loss of a parent. So you, as the surviving parent, may be forced to repeat painful details over and over again, and be thrust in the role of comforter at times when it is difficult to cope with your own grief.

Additional losses, such as the loss of a pet, or a house, or even a simple family tradition may cause the grief to rise to the surface again, prompting a stronger than anticipated reaction. At such times, the parent who recognizes and takes steps to acknowledge the source of the problem helps that child find the healing as he moves from anger to acceptance.

How have you seen these "cycles of grief" operate in your own children?

_____

_____

_____

_____

_____

_____

_____

❦ PRAYER OF THE DAY ❦

Mother Mary, Exalted Widow, pray for me that I might have supernatural strength to revisit that "valley of the shadow" with my children until we find our way back to the light.

Psalm 31:8-13

*I will rejoice and be glad in your love, once you have seen
my misery, observed my distress.*

*You will not abandon me into enemy hands,
but will set my feet in a free and open space.*

*Be gracious to me, LORD, for I am in distress;
with grief my eyes are wasted, my soul and body spent.*

*My life is worn out by sorrow, my years by sighing.
My strength fails in affliction; my bones are consumed.*

*To all my foes I am a thing of scorn, to my neighbors, a
dreaded sight, a horror to my friends. When they see me in
the street, they quickly shy away.*

*I am forgotten, out of mind like the dead; I am like a
shattered dish.*

♡ PRAYER OF THE DAY ♡

This psalm contains several powerful images that are apt metaphors for the feelings associated with the loss of a loved one. Which one strikes closest to home for you?

Write your own psalm to God.

_____

_____

_____

_____

ALTARS OF GOD:
WIDOWS IN THE EARLY CHURCH

*"Older women should be reverent in their behavior, not slanderers,
not addicted to drink, teaching what is good, so that they may
train younger women to love their husbands and children, to be
self-controlled, chaste, good homemakers, under the control of their
husbands, so that the word of God may not be discredited."*

Titus 2:3-5

*"Let not the widows be wanderers about, nor fond of dainties, nor
gadders from house to house; but let them be like Judith, noted for
her seriousness; and like Anna, eminent for her sobriety."*

Ignatius of Antioch
As quoted in *The Widows*

Polycarp, Bishop of Smyrna, was enjoined by Ignatius to be the guardian of widows. In his own writings Polycarp describes the widow as "an altar of God." As altars of God, widows were to avoid all evil, including love of money. They were to intercede for all, in the spirit not of Martha but of Mary. Christian widows – pagans referred to them as "old hags," suggesting that they were not well dressed – prayed in front of jails where Christians were being detained or tortured.

One theologian of early Church days mentions that a chaste widow is especially to be honored in a way different from virgins because "it is easy not to crave after that which you know not, and to turn away from what you have never had to regret." The same theologian warns against drink and curiosity. Instead the widow should be occupied with counsel and comfort.

The image of the widow as an altar of God includes the concept of the burnt offering, obeying God and sacrificing of herself by giving service to the community and also avoiding sinful or scandalous behavior. The *Didache* also describes widows as in the likeness of the altar. It states that no widow under fifty years of age may join the "order" of widows, lest she later marry and cause scandal or deplete the Church's resources when she is marriageable.

The bishop was responsible for assuring support for widows and orphans, and was to make certain the benefactors were honorable in their intentions. Widows were not to teach the faith in the way that Jesus appointed the apostles to do, nor were they to baptize. Instead they were to pray, do good works (including making clothes, working at wool, and visiting), lay hands on the sick, and fast. They are not to visit homes without permission of the hierarchy. Widows were exhorted to be meek and quiet and gentle, not chatterers.

❦ FOR PONDERING ❦

Polycarp described a widow as "an altar of God." What does this mean to you? How does this phrase help set a standard for a godly lifestyle? What areas do you need to work on to conform to this standard?

_____

_____

_____

_____

_____

_____

❦ PRAYER OF THE DAY ❦

Lord, when I am tempted to "chatter," may I always take that opportunity to whisper in Your ear.

BLESSED ANGELA OF FOLIGNO: "WAY OF PENANCE"

Keep our life all spotless,
Make our way secure,
Till we find in Jesus,
Joy forevermore.

Through the highest heaven
To the Almighty Three,
Father, Son and Spirit,
One same glory be. Amen.
"Ave Maris Stella" (9th Century)

In 1285, she began to fear damnation – and it was the start of her conversion. Weeping bitterly, Angela was too ashamed to tell the priest every sin in confession, and consequently she was receiving Holy Communion sacrilegiously. In prayer she begged Saint Francis to find her a worthy confessor, and she found a good one who absolved her of all her sins. She gave her property to the poor and adopted the habit of the Third Order of Saint Francis.

On pilgrimage to Assisi, Blessed Angela begged for the grace to feel Christ's presence in her soul and to observe the rule perfectly. It was at a wayside shrine that she had an extraordinary grace in an experience of the Trinity. On the same pilgrimage, sensing Christ's presence in an intense way, she became afraid of losing this loving tender feeling, and she threw herself on the floor of the Basilica of Saint Francis shouting in an unintelligible way. Her confessor, Arnaldo, told her not to come back.

For several years Blessed Angela experienced great joy and peace from the graces of the pilgrimage. When Arnaldo was assigned to Foligno, he questioned her about her behavior, thinking it was caused by demons, but gradually became so impressed that he became her scribe.

After this relatively happy period of divine revelations and ecstatic visions, in 1294 Angela began to experience despair and abandonment as well as intimacy and union. She felt both chosen and damned. She had to struggle with terrible demonic temptations.

The last thirteen years of her life were spent primarily in being a spiritual mother to a small community that gathered around her. Her teachings are assembled in the book called *Instructions.* On her deathbed she said that Christ had come to tell her that He would come for her Himself.

We now turn to specific quotations from *The Memorial,* and the "way of penance" that Blessed Angela dictated to Brother Arnaldo. Her penitential path predates her widowhood. However, it was intensified after she was free "to leave the world."

I find Angela's way of penance difficult, though inspiring, reading. There was a time when the idea of penance was repugnant in the extreme, since daily life seemed difficult enough without adding anything. However, I now recognize the way of penance to be simply and consciously accepting both the little and the terrible sufferings of life, and offering them to Christ generously, in reparation for sin. Each of these steps takes time. The soul is sluggish, and moves so painfully and ponderously toward God. It takes such tiny steps at a time.

Steps 1-2: Awareness and confession of sin. As the soul grows in awareness of sin, it "weeps bitterly" with shame and bitterness. There is not yet the feeling of love, only grief. She [Blessed Angela] told me how she had often received communion in a state of sin because she had been too ashamed to make a full confession.

Steps 3-4: Penance begins. The soul performs penance in satisfaction to God for its sins; it is still grief-stricken but grows in awareness of Divine Mercy. The soul...[is granted awareness of] forgiveness, begins to be enlightened, and then weeps and grieves even more than before, and undertakes even sharper penance.

Steps 5-6: Knowledge of my self, and of the depths of my sin. Here the soul sees nothing but defects in itself, and recognizes how God has been offended. Blessed Angela is quoted as saying, "I was given to pray with a great fire of love invoking all the saints and the Blessed Virgin.... As a result, it did seem to me that all creatures had mercy on me, and all the saints."

Steps 7-8: Seeing the crucified Christ, and being crucified with Him. "In the seventh step I was given the grace of beginning to look at the cross... I felt that I myself had crucified Christ. … Standing near the cross, I stripped myself of all my clothing and offered my whole self to him. Although very fearful, I promised him then to maintain perpetual chastity … on the one hand, I feared to make this promise, but on the other hand, the fire of which I spoke drew it out of me, and I could not do otherwise."

Steps 9-10: Seek the way of the cross. "This would entail forgiving all who had offended me, stripping myself of everything worldly, of all attachments to men and women, of my friends and relatives, and everyone else, and, likewise, of my possessions and even my very self. … [Christ] appeared to me many times, both while I was asleep and awake, crucified on the cross. He told me that I should look at his wounds. [He showed her how each wound was incurred for her sins.]...I wept much, shedding such hot tears that they burned my flesh. I had to apply water to cool it."

Steps 11-12: Harsher penance. Here the translator mentions that the type of penances performed during this period of Church history included such practices as praying with arms outstretched for long periods, wearing iron chains and hair shirts, flagellating oneself, and fasting on bread and water for long periods of time. Angela decided to live as much as possible in total poverty in spite of fear of hunger, cold, and nakedness. She resolved to trust that even if she died of such privations, she would be happy in God.

Steps 13-14: Entering into the Passion and kissing the wounds of Christ. [Here Angela entered into the] sorrow over the passion suffered by the mother of Christ and Saint John. She came to love the heart of Christ. "He called me to place my mouth to the wound in his side. It seemed to me that I saw and drank the blood, which was freshly flowing from his side." This blood was to cleanse her. She felt great joy at this blessing but at the same time sadness about the passion and a desire to suffer as he did.

Steps 15-16: More sorrow and penance. Here Angela understands what John experienced of sorrow at the crucifixion (see John 19:26-27); this gave her a greater resolve to get rid of her possessions no matter what her mentors said to dissuade her; still she felt no relief, only bitter sorrow for her sins. In the next step, Angela was able to understand the meaning of each line of the Our Father, and she began to know the divine sweetness in meditating on the goodness of God.

Steps 17-18: Conversion and "fire." Angela sees that it was Mary who obtained for her the grace of conversion; she receives consolation in dreams and visions and a grace of continual divine sweetness. She felt such joy in prayer that she forgot to eat, and wished she did not need to eat; but she saw that it was a temptation not to eat. "The fire in my heart became so intense that if I heard anyone speak about God I would scream."

People thought her possessed. Her woman companion had to hide paintings of the passion to stop her from running a fever when contemplating them.

Steps 19-20: Betrothed to the Holy Spirit. Angela went into an ecstacy from contemplating the divinity and humanity of Christ. Brother Arnaldo relates how he came to know Blessed Angela, and started writing down an account of her experiences. Of special note in the narratives that follow are these:

- The promise of the Holy Spirit to be with her forever as her spouse, more beloved than anyone in the Valley of Spoleto because of her total surrender to Christ: "I am much more prepared to give than you are to receive."

- That penance is always accompanied by tremendous joyful graces.

- On receiving graces of great love from the Holy Spirit in the Church of Saint Francis in Assisi, Angela felt pain when Jesus withdrew from her. "Love still unknown, why do you leave me?" she shouted out. "Why? Why? Why?"

- On the road home, Jesus said, "Your whole life, your eating, drinking, sleeping, and all that you do are pleasing to me."

For eight days Blessed Angela experienced such intimacy with God that her scribe describes it as "mystical betrothal." Blessed Angela observed, "We have no excuse for not receiving Christ's love. We should come to him humbly as a sick person goes to the doctor and, revealing our illness, open ourselves to the doctor's remedy."

❦ FOR REFLECTION AND DISCUSSION ❦

Which of Blessed Angela's steps resonate with you? Why?

_____

_____

_____

_____

_____

_____

Which steps do not resonate with you? Why?

_____

_____

_____

_____

_____

_____

Which steps do you think God is asking you to incorporate into your life now?

_____

_____

_____

_____

_____

_____

Develop a practical strategy to incorporate one of the steps identified above. Move forward with your plan today.

_____

_____

_____

_____

_____

_____

❦ PRAYER OF THE DAY ❦

Keep our life all spotless,
Make our way secure,
Till we find in Jesus,
Joy forevermore.

Through the highest heaven
To the Almighty Three,
Father, Son and Spirit,
One same glory be. Amen.

CHAPTER TWELVE

CRY OF ANTICIPATION

Twelfth Station
Jesus Dies on the Cross

Mary …

How often the ways of God must have surprised you, from the Annunciation on through all the mysteries of your life. Perhaps as Jesus was being crucified you waited expectantly for another miracle, hoping that somehow the resurrection would occur right then.

But that did not happen. Instead Jesus gave you another unexpected gift: the gift of spiritual motherhood. You were to become mother of His Church, symbolized in the person of John, the beloved apostle.

Jesus, even in the last moments, we prayed for our husband's healing and health. Even when they died suddenly, without warning, we prayed over their bodies hoping that they, like Lazarus, could be raised from the dead. We wanted them to remain with us here on earth.

As we pray for the souls of our husbands, we are reminded that there is still work that You have for us to do. As we mourn, let our tears never blind us to the need for love in the people around us.

❦ FOR PONDERING ❦

As you think about your life and gifts, how is God calling you to "spiritual motherhood" now, in your widowhood?

_____

_____

_____

_____

_____

_____

❦ PRAYER OF THE DAY ❦

Walk with me, Jesus ... (insert your own prayer here)

_____

_____

_____

_____

_____

_____

_____

_____

_____

Concepcion Cabrera de Armida:
Loving God ... and Family

"A powerful grace impels me to undertake, in my new state of life, a new way of perfection, of sacrifice, of solitude, of hidden life.... I understand that the Lord wants to purify me that I may be more His."
From the diary of the newly widowed Conchita

Concepcion Cabrera de Armida (Conchita) was a "contemplative in the world" whose story will have great appeal for widows who — however ardently called to a life of prayer — will never live in a convent.

Born in 1862 in San Luis Portosi, Mexico, this Mexican holy woman kept journals in which we find an articulate expression of why she thought that a happy marriage was a supernatural vocation. Conchita was extremely religious as a girl, but she longed to be married and have children. "Lord, I feel so unable to love you, so I want to get married. Give me many children so that they will love you better than I," she would pray.

In those days engagements lasted a long time. Conchita was engaged for about nine years, from the age of thirteen until she was twenty-two. She tried always to love her fiancé not in an exclusively natural way but rather to love him in God. She saw no conflict between love of God and love for her Pancho.

Very happily married, Conchita and Pancho had nine children, and yet she still spent much time in prayer, especially making intercession for priests. After the sudden death of her husband, when Conchita still had to care for small children, she took over the administration of family matters. Gradually, with the help of a holy priest, she laid the foundation for several orders devoted to what she called the "Works of the Cross." These apostolates include the Sisters of the Cross, the Missionaries of the Holy Spirit, and associations of laypeople. The Holy Spirit instructed the foundress not to become a member herself of the contemplative order of sisters but to remain in the world as a woman consecrated interiorly to Christ.

More than a hundred volumes of her writings exist in the Spanish language, so there are many who think that when she is canonized she will also be added to the names of Saints Catherine of Siena and Teresa of Avila as a Doctor of the Church. The following are passages from her journals for you to ponder.

"While riding about the countryside with my father and my sister, Clara, I spent hours reflecting on how I could manage to live in a mountain cave all by myself, far from everyone, giving myself up to penance and prayer whenever the spirit moved me. I was delighted at the thought and pondered it in my heart ... I would ride along meditating very slowly, word for word, prayers to our Blessed Sacrament or to the Blessed Virgin ... my childish heart found ineffable delight in all this."

When still a young girl, obliged to go to dances and the theater, Conchita felt drawn ever more into a life of prayer:

"At the heart of this ocean of vanities and festivals, I felt within my soul a burning desire to learn how to pray....I kept myself as much as I could in God's presence. This was enough [for me] to begin seeing a great light shed on the nothingness of worldly things, on the vanity of existence, on the beauty of God.... Christ drew me to himself, absorbed me, enchanted me."

❦ FOR PONDERING ❦

"It is only in My crucified Heart that the ineffable sweetness of My Heart can be tasted," she heard Christ say to her. "Seen from the outside, the Cross is bitter and harsh, but ... there is no greater pleasure. Therein is the repose of the soul, the soul inebriated by love, therein its delights, its life."

This last quote is especially relevant to the life of the newly widowed. "From the outside, the Cross is bitter and harsh, but there is no greater pleasure…."

Have you found this to be true in your own life? Write about it.

_____

_____

_____

_____

_____

_____

_____

✄ PRAYER OF THE DAY ✄

Jesus,
my bitter made sweet,
my pain made joyful,
my death eternal life.
Give me the courage to see with the eyes of faith
all the good You want for me.

JESUS THE BRIDEGROOM:
ON MYSTICAL UNION

"Here I am, I want to incarnate Myself mystically in your heart....
Receive Me.... I have taken possession of your heart...."

Christ to Conchita

Studying the biography of Concepcion Cabrera de Armida, or Conchita, we find a special way of encountering Christ as the Bridegroom-Savior — being drawn oneself into union with Christ's saving passion. The description to follow may provide you with a poignant sense of how far He could be leading each of us also if we were sufficiently generous of heart.

Shortly before the feast of the Annunciation, when Conchita was forty years old, Jesus began to prepare her in prayer for what she says He called the "mystical incarnation." During a retreat, before the feast, Conchita felt great anguish for the salvation of souls. She made a general confession of all the faults of her life.

Then, on the morning of the feast, after a night spent in prayer and penance, at Mass she felt herself taken over by the presence of Christ, who said to her: "Here I am, I want to incarnate Myself mystically in your heart.... Receive Me.... I have taken possession of your heart...."

She asked if this was the spiritual marriage. He replied: "Much more than that. Marriage is a form of more external union; the grace of incarnating Me, of living and growing in your soul, never to leave it, to possess you and to be possessed by you as in one and the same substance, without, obviously, you giving Me life; rather, it is I who communicate it to your soul in a compenetration which cannot be comprehended: it is the grace of graces.... It is a union of the same nature as that of the union of heaven, except that in paradise the veil which conceals the Divinity disappears...."

Conchita felt a sublime sense of Christ living in her soul, but she asked just the same: "'Lord, what if this was a figment of my imagination or a delusion?' He replied, 'You will discern all that from the results flowing therefrom...no one merits it. Love Me. This kind of union is most profound, most intimate and, if your soul remains faithful, it will be an internal union.'"

Conchita wrote that, after this experience, "I felt my spirit inundated with freshness, peace, infinite delights, but was it true? Yes, certainly, year after year I saw myself humiliated by this promise, which apparently was never carried out. I did not understand it all. My tears flowed.... Behold, the handmaid of the Lord. Be it done unto me according to Thy Word."

The form that this mystical incarnation was to take was to urge Conchita on to be a victim for the Church in union with Christ — Priest and Host. It was to be a path of suffering, lived in fidelity to each inspiration of the Holy Spirit. She was to offer herself on the altar in union with Christ, through which thousands and thousands of souls will be saved. Her biographer writes: "This mystical incarnation eminently realized the 'royal priesthood' of all the members of the family of Christ."

❦ PRAYER OF THE DAY ❦

Pray now with Conchita: *"Here I am, I want to incarnate Myself mystically in your heart.... Receive Me.... I have taken possession of your heart...."*

Psalm 21:3-7

You have granted him his heart's desire;
you did not refuse the prayer of his lips. Selah

For you welcomed him with goodly blessings;
you placed on his head a crown of pure gold.

He asked life of you;
you gave it to him, length of days forever.

Great is his glory in your victory;
majesty and splendor you confer upon him.

You make him the pattern of blessings forever,
you gladden him with the joy of your presence.

ॐ FOR PONDERING ॐ

As our Second Bridegroom beckons to us, calls us to plunge ever deeper into His Sacred Heart, we turn and contemplate the joy that must be even greater than our own: the joy of those who have at last received their "heart's desire" and stand in glorious splendor, basking in the never-ending radiance of the One who made them, redeemed them, and who calls them by name.

One day this joy will be ours. Our heart's desire will be fulfilled as we are reunited with those we love … especially that one person who loved us best in this world.

"He asked life of you; you gave it to him, length of days forever."

To what extent does this thought bring you consolation?

_____

_____

_____

_____

_____

_____

_____

_____

_____

_____

_____

_____

_____

❦ PRAYER OF THE DAY ❦

Lord, my beloved could not remain here on earth with me as long as we would have liked; and yet, in just a little while we shall never again be parted. Selah!

A Widow's Story:
Ronda and Alice on Regret

"I believe that I shall see the bounty of the Lord in the land of the living.
Wait for the Lord with courage; be stouthearted, and wait for the Lord."
Psalm 27:13-14

For some widows, death is sudden and unwelcome – like a thief in the night. For others, especially for those who have suffered through a spouse's prolonged illness, death is something of a relief. Others struggle with mixed feelings: regret over past conflicts, relief over the end of the struggle, possibly even guilty thoughts of remarriage.

In my case, I had been anticipating my husband's death for a long time. And because our marriage had not exactly been the stuff of fairy tales, when he died I had already harbored thoughts of second husbands. But gradually, over many years, I came to miss my husband very much for his virtues. Being rid of his faults removed pain, but it didn't bring joy. But his virtues such as joy in life, or his love of the arts, I did (and still do) miss.

If you harbor similar feelings of regret, you may find comfort in these words:

Don't dwell on the mistakes and failings in your marriage. Beg God for forgiveness but don't think they mean all the good memories were illusory. When you recall these failures, ask for the grace to become now the person God wishes you to be and your husband wished also. Not only God forgives you but also your husband since he now is in the world of the redeemed.

Alice von Hildebrand
By Grief Refined

❦ FOR REFLECTION AND DISCUSSION ❦

Do you find yourself harboring regrets, for not having built up your husband and your marriage with greater patience, greater tolerance, greater love? Can you think of some specific examples?

_____

_____

_____

_____

_____

Do you feel there is a kind of barrier between you and your spouse in eternity because of past conflicts? You might try writing him a letter, or having a conversation with him in which you ask forgiveness for whatever was your part of those conflicts. Ask him from Purgatory or Heaven to pray for you to become more the woman God wants.

❦ PRAYER OF THE DAY ❦

Imagine your husband sitting opposite you. How would you complete these statements?

My darling, forgive me for …
I'm so thankful for …
Please pray for me, for …

Jesus, some of us had wonderful marriages and our grief in widowhood is piercing but pure. Others of us had such difficulties that our feelings are mixed. The shock of death can leave even the most devout Catholic survivors with doubts about life after death or the eternal salvation of their spouse. Jesus, Bridegroom of Widows, help us. Mary, Exalted Widow help us, widow saints help us.

St. Jane de Chantal:
Experiencing the Love of Christ

"When the Holy Spirit has taken possession of the person who prays, it does as it pleases without any more need for rules and methods.... Prayer must happen by grace, not by artfulness..."

St. Jane de Chantal

Experiencing Christ as the Bridegroom and the true Lover of her heart and soul was for St. Jane de Chantal mediated by the love she found in the friendship of the holy St. Francis de Sales. Pledging to help her toward spiritual growth, despite her distressing circumstances as a widow living in worldly and sinful surroundings, St. Francis expressed himself with compelling ardor: "I am all yours... God has given me to you; so consider me as yours in Him, and call me whatever you like; it makes no difference."

For someone accustomed to natural human love as a happily married woman, opening to this distinctly Christian but ardently overflowing love from a holy man seems to have been the key to the new spirituality she was called to embrace. Before this friendship, Jane's way to God was somewhat stiff and formal even though characterized by surrender of the will and total commitment to executing the will of God in prayer and love of neighbor. De Sales recommended instead walking in the presence of God with absolute liberty of spirit.

By freedom of spirit, of course, De Sales did not mean "freedom to sin." Rather, he wanted Jane to know more joy in her Second Bridegroom, because he was convinced that no deprivation can sadden the heart that belongs wholly to God. Little inconveniences or trifles do not upset such a Christian. Interruptions make no difference. Those with liberty of spirit are rarely angry and almost always serene.

Enchanted by the personal love Francis had for her whole person, as a woman of God, Jane could allow herself to be receptive to Christ the Second Bridegroom in quite a new way. In her own letters of spiritual direction, Jane de Chantal could recommend that "the great method of prayer is to have no method at all. When the Holy Spirit has taken possession of the person who prays, it does as it pleases without any more need for rules and methods.... Prayer must happen by grace, not by artfulness."

Yet, characteristically, there comes a time on the path of total surrender to Jesus when even attachment to holy people has to give way to complete reliance on Christ alone. Francis promised Jane that one day he would detach her even from himself. ... She struggled to reduce all her desires to the desire for unity with God in acceptance of his will. This is a kind of bridal spiritual nakedness in relationship to Jesus the Second Bridegroom.

At the time of Francis' death, our French widow-saint replied to her brother's letter of condolence with the following words:

You say you want to know what my heart felt on that occasion. Ah, it seems to me that it adored God in the profound silence of its terrible anguish. Truly, I have never felt such an intense grief nor has my spirit ever received so heavy a blow ... the only thing that is left to console me is to know that it is my God that has done this, or at least, has permitted this blow to fall. Alas. My heart is too weak to support this heavy burden ... Yes, my God, you put this beautiful soul into the world, now you have taken it back ... may the name of the Lord be blessed.... I affirm what it has pleased Him to do — to take from us that great flame that lit up this miserable world and let it shine in his kingdom.... I am certainly too insignificant to merit such a great blessing as well as the contentment that I had in seeing my soul held in the hands of such a great man who was truly a man of God.

❦ FOR REFLECTION AND DISCUSSION ❦

"You put this beautiful soul into the world, now you have taken it back ... may the name of the Lord be blessed." This heartfelt prayer is a courageous confession that may be offered back to God in all kinds of circumstances. The loss of a spouse, certainly. But the loss of other dear souls as well ... parents, siblings – even children.

Notice how the detachment of which St. Jane speaks of in this passage contrasts to the spiritual attachment she had formed with St. Francis de

Sales. God did not leave her bereft of all support and encouragement. He sent her ... not a romantic soul mate, but something even better: a true friend who understood the deepest intentions of her heart even better (at times) than she did herself.

Do you think this kind of friendship is something to aspire to, or seek out? Why or why not?

_____

_____

_____

_____

_____

_____

_____

_____

Chapter Thirteen

CRY OF INTERCESSION

Thirteenth Station
Jesus Is Taken from the Cross

Mary …

Great artists and sculptors have depicted the tender moment when you held the body of Jesus for the last time. Did you also remember holding the body of St. Joseph for the last time? How often we wish that we could see our husbands again in the flesh, and embrace them in love.

Pray for us, O Holy Mary, that we might offer these longings back to God. Turn our grief into powerful seeds of prayer.

Jesus, You want us to grieve but not to beg for what is not Your will. Instead of physical contact with our husband's bodies, You want to stretch us to make contact with them through prayer. Please wean us from wanting what is gone and help us to want what we can have in a spiritual way now, and in eternity. Some widows experience the souls of their spouses with them always, and others, rarely, if at all. Help us to trust in the signs of eternal life You choose for each of us as individuals. Many of us have found healing graces through groups on bereavement and grief. If we could benefit from such ministries, help us to overcome our desire to hide our pain. Let us not reject what would bring hope.

ॐ FOR PONDERING ॐ

How has your grief changed your perspective on eternal life (life after
death), if at all?

_____

_____

_____

_____

_____

_____

_____

ॐ PRAYER OF THE DAY ॐ

Walk with me, Jesus ... (insert your own prayer here)

_____

_____

_____

_____

_____

_____

_____

_____

BLESSED CONCHITA:
WORKS OF THE CROSS

"I sense His presence, above all on receiving Communion, flooding me with His light, with His rays and purifying me ... he impels me, by the acceptance of sacrifice, to crucify myself, to desire suffering, martyrdom, to give my blood every day for the salvation of souls."
Blessed Conchita

After her marriage, Conchita continued a life of constant prayer and penance, and was gradually drawn into the prayer of quiet. Christ told her that her mission would be to save souls. The opportunity came at the farm of a relative where she was staying. She brought together sixty women of the town and began to teach them about the spiritual life.

She began to thirst for the salvation of souls, and finally got her director's permission to engrave the initials of the holy name of Jesus, IHS (actually the abbreviation of the Greek word for Jesus), on her bosom. She wanted to feel "branded," belonging totally to Jesus. She felt spiritually wed to him, and longed to sacrifice all for Christ. ...

Even before she became a widow, during her many visions of the Cross, Conchita saw interiorly a procession of nuns bearing a great red cross. This was the first intimation that she would found an order of Sisters of the Cross. According to her, the Lord also announced that there would be a congregation of men.

The Missionaries of the Holy Spirit was to be an order of priests dedicated, among many sacramental works, to offering their own sufferings for other priests. During this time nine volumes written about her life, based on her spiritual diary, were examined by the Vatican. She was summoned to go to Rome herself for a personal interview with Pope Pius X and with the Congregation for Religious. The Holy Father gave her a special blessing and told her that he had approved all the Works of the Cross, asking her to pray for him. During her interview with the monsignor from the congregation she begged that she herself might remain in a hidden life in the world and not live in any of the religious orders.

The approvals were granted eighteen years after her first visions and locutions concerning these foundations. Addressing Jesus, she wrote: "What pains, sufferings, penances, disappointments! What blood, prayers, calumnies, feelings of envy, persecutions, and tears all this has cost. But it all is as nothing when I think that it was for purifying Your Works for Your greater glory."

The last twenty years of her life saw Conchita's children grown up and her own life more and more one of solitude. Her external works diminished and her prayer life became more one of abandonment and immolation with an apparent remoteness of God, similar to that of Jesus on the Cross.

About this period she wrote: "I am in the most complete solitude of soul, but it is God's will and God, for me, is only there where His will is found. I do not understand anything any more. I am in chaos. This need to express my soul, my desires, my impressions, even on paper, all this has disappeared. I tend to keep secret my impressions, my tastes and even my sufferings and tears. I want to hide everything in Jesus. All is for Him alone.... On the earth, all is shadow, vanity and lies. The real, the true, what is of value, what endures, what is, is in heaven. The earth with all its things, all of them, are but a lever to raise oneself to Him...if I consult my heart, I discover its affections. They have passed. Its desires, the most ardent ones, its excessive yearnings for such and such a thing, have passed.... I ardently desired to be a nun, now that is all the same to me: to be or not to be, to die here or there....I have only one desire: that in me the divine will be done."

It is in the story of Conchita that we find a particularly inspiring form of sacrificial love. Despite the obstacles and difficulties she experienced in carrying out God's plan for her, this Mexican widow-saint devoted herself to prayer and penance for the most sinful members of the clergy.

Shortly after her husband's death, Conchita met the holy priest with whom she would co-found several religious orders. An interior sense led her to visit a particular church for confession. She opened to this priest her whole soul, especially about her sense of the delight of suffering with Christ on the Cross, and her belief that she was called to promote a spiritual path called the Works of the Cross. This priest, Father Felix Rougier, who had experienced the same calling himself, became her spiritual director. His cause for beatification is being considered together with that of Conchita.

This friendship was itself nailed to the Cross, for Father Felix's superiors thought that he should not associate with such a woman mystic. He was exiled for ten years to Europe, where he served in lowly capacities.

Conchita's biographer remarks that Father Felix was not a dreamer but a mature, realistic person with a rocklike strength. He was a great help to her in founding several orders, exchanging advice and encouragement along the path of holiness.

♥ FOR REFLECTION AND DISCUSSION ♥

Conchita was a woman who loved God, and loved her family. Like many women, she experienced the "pull" between the conflicting demands of family life and spiritual life. Have you ever felt this way? In what ways have you tried to resolve these conflicts?

_____

_____

_____

_____

_____

_____

_____

_____

_____

SAINT BRIGID OF SWEDEN
SAINT IN HIGH SOCIETY

Saint Brigid of Sweden (1323-1373) was born to pious parents of high rank in Swedish society. The night Brigid was born, the priest saw a vision of the Blessed Virgin Mary, who said to him that Brigid's "wondrous voice shall be heard all over the world." God used Brigid's knowledge of the life of the court so that she might play a prophetic role in these influential circles. It was she who suggested that the Scriptures be translated into Swedish.

Although Brigid wanted to be a nun, she willingly agreed to marry Prince Ulf at the age of fourteen. She loved him dearly, and bore him four sons and four daughters. They were happily married for twenty-eight years.

Brigid was a Third Order Franciscan. In penitential style, she wore a hair shirt under her fashionable courtly clothing and exercised a prophetic ministry by challenging society people to live according to the Gospel. It was during this time that Christ appeared to Brigid and told her to form a double monastery of nuns and monks at Vadstena: "Thou shalt not only be counted my bride, but also a nun and mother in Vadstena."

On pilgrimages with her husband, Brigid felt a great yearning to become a contemplative nun, but Christ told her that even when she became a widow he wanted her to remain in court, in order to convert her relatives and friends.

During the period before the death of her husband, innumerable miracles of healing and exorcisms were attributed to her touch. Brigid spoke up against the murder, looting, rape, and unnatural sexual sins that were rampant in Sweden in those times. Long afterward, in Rome and Naples, she would also prophesy against abortion and slavery.

She lived in Rome during the years of the Avignon papacy, and the Lord showed her that she was to try to reconcile the Avignon pope with the emperor. She was a faithful intercessor in the pilgrim churches for many years, and eventually saw Charles IV accompany Pope Urban back to Rome from France.

As a widow, St. Brigid had many visions in which saints appeared and advised her on how to conduct her life. In one vision Saint Agnes showed her how important it was that she use her scholarship to defend the truth through Scripture rather than stay home and spin.

In another vision, the Blessed Virgin told Brigid that she must write to a cardinal to tell him about how the Church was being ruined by the sexual sins and greediness of many ecclesiastics, with the assurance that God would grace those who repaired such damage.

At one point Christ told the Swedish saint to leave Rome and visit a monastery infamous for moral abuses. There Jesus compelled her to denounce the abbot about his womanizing, accusing him of being a father to his own children instead of being a father to the poor.

Brigid became well-known in Rome for her prophecies against the evils of the Church. The common people, who lived in fear of poverty and the plague, decided St. Brigid was the source of these evils. Carrying flaming torches they gathered in the square of the cardinal's palace, yelling that "the witch should leave" and the house burned. The priest barred the door, the cook was terrified, and the women wept. Concerned that she was endangering the pilgrims around her, Brigid went to the oratory and asked Christ what to do. Christ told her she must stay, and little harm was done.

On pilgrimage to the Holy Land, Brigid received many revelations from the Virgin Mary about the Nativity, the Immaculate Conception, and the Assumption. Her visions of the mysteries of the Passion greatly influenced Catholic art and music. The famous revelations about the sufferings of Christ in his Passion are still being distributed for devotional purposes today.

❦ FOR REFLECTION AND DISCUSSION ❦

The Lord commanded St. Brigid to retain her position in society in order to influence her peers with the truths of the Gospel. What does her fidelity to this calling say to us today? In what ways can we be a "voice for the Gospel" in our own day?

_____

_____

_____

_____

Psalm 42:2-7

As the deer longs for streams of water,
so my soul longs for you, O God.
My being thirsts for God, the living God.
When can I go and see the face of God?

My tears have been my food day and night,
as they ask daily, "Where is your God?"

Those times I recall as I pour out my soul,
When I went in procession with the crowd, I went with them
to the house of God, Amid loud cries of thanksgiving,
with the multitude keeping festival.

Why are you downcast, my soul; why do you groan within me?
Wait for God, whom I shall praise again, my savior and my God.

ಠಿ FOR PONDERING ಠಿ

"Amid loud cries of thanksgiving, with the multitude keeping festival, why are you downcast, my soul?"

What do you have to be thankful for today?

_____

_____

_____

_____

_____

_____

WHAT CAN I DO?

"I am confident of this, that the one who began a good work in you will continue to complete it until the day of Christ Jesus."

Philippians 1:6

Some widows sink into a miserable sense that God has nothing left for them to do after their spouse dies. In reality, lay widows have many avenues of service within their families, society, and in the Church. The change in their state in life often represents an opportunity to experiment.

Some widow saints became religious sisters and even founded new orders; this shows us that with courage we can respond to the surprising graces God wants to send each of us.

For example, Blessed Maria Domenica Brun Barbantini (1789-1868) was widowed only six months after she married at twenty-two. She gave birth to their child, a boy, whom she raised (he died when he was eight years old). She also took over her husband's business and helped the needy, forming a group of women called the Pious Union of the Sisters of Charity. She actively promoted what was called Catholic Action. In 1829, a priest helped Blessed Maria found the Sister Servants of the Sick of Saint Camillus.

One lovely thing about being a widow is more time for quiet prayer. I love the Liturgy of the Hours. You can find information online and in books about how to pray this morning, midday, evening, and night. One website you may find helpful is the St. Thomas More House of Prayer website (http://www.liturgyofthehours.org), particularly the "resources" section.

❦ FOR PONDERING ❦

Of the many opportunities we have examined here, which ones have you tried? Are there any outreaches or services people ask you to perform that you might want to try with the greater amount of time you have since your husband left this world?

_____

_____

_____

_____

_____

_____

_____

_____

_____

For more information about options for widows, lay and consecrated, go to www.rondachervin.com and click on "widows."

PRAXEDES FERNANDEZ:
REVOLUTION OF LOVE

"What good is it, my brothers, if someone says he has faith but does not have works? Can that faith save him? If a brother or sister has nothing to wear and has no food for the day, and one of you says to them, "Go in peace, keep warm, and eat well," but you do not give them the necessities of the body, what good is it? So also faith of itself, if it does not have works, is dead."

James 2:14-17

When the Communist revolution in Spain erupted, Praxedes Fernandez found herself living in a Communist-dominated parish. Because of the violence, the bishop sent the parish priest away ... and yet these same people who refused to have anything to do with the Church, loved Praxedes for her charity to one and all. She would help those who supported the Church as well as those who hated it. "If all Catholics were like Praxedes," they would say, "then we would believe in religion."

During the revolution, Praxedes began to attend three Masses a day: one to prepare for Communion, the second for actually receiving Communion, and the third for giving thanks. At these Masses she was given many graces, especially the assurance of the salvation of her deceased husband and son.

When all the priests were massacred or exiled, Praxedes went from house to house baptizing babies, comforting the sick, and preparing the dying for their final journey. As the violence increased, Praxedes dedicated her life to penance for her country. "All this is happening because there is no prayer life and there are no sacrifices in the lives of the people," she used to say. Praxedes knew that voluntary suffering, accepted and joined to that of Jesus, contributes to the salvation of the world.

Praxedes' works of mercy increased as the poverty and suffering caused by the war increased. She was called "the Mother of the poor." Besides her corporal works of mercy, her very presence was a grace to others. Maintaining her calm amidst bombings, she assured those hiding in her home that there was nothing to fear. Only the loss of souls was important.

She refused to let anyone pass harsh judgment on Communists, instead praying for their conversion.

During this time she became a Third Order Dominican, taking the name Catalina in honor of Saint Catherine of Siena.

In 1934, the whole family moved into a larger house in another town where there was still sacramental life. Now she could receive Holy Communion often. The prophetic gift became strong in the spirit of Praxedes, who predicted another war. In 1935, she offered herself as a victim of reparation for the future war. But Praxedes also predicted that the Blessed Virgin would be with us, and that the Sacred Heart would eventually triumph.

In 1936, while nursing the sick during a typhoid epidemic, Praxedes contracted the disease herself. So peacefully did she die that those around her couldn't believe she was dead. The humble violet was finally buried in the garden of her beloved.

❦ FOR REFLECTION AND DISCUSSION ❦

How have you been expressing faith through your actions?

_____

_____

_____

_____

_____

❦ PRAYER OF THE DAY ❦

Lord, I want my faith to remain active and vital. Give me opportunities to exercise it today!

CHAPTER FOURTEEN

CRY OF REUNION

Fourteenth Station
Jesus Is Buried

Mary …

Some who write about you believe that Jesus first appeared to you, His mother, privately. We do not know how that was, but we do know that you understand how we feel at the burial of those we love. Even with the numbness that often comes with a death, the farewell at the gravesite is always poignant.

Jesus, You want to increase our faith in life eternal. In the meantime, You teach us to believe in Your mystical body, experienced in its highest form on earth at Holy Mass and in the reception of Holy Communion. Help us to believe that our communion with You at the sacred rites is also a communion with the one to whom we were joined in the sacrament of marriage. You have made saints of some widows, known to us, or hidden from the public eye. What more can we pray for than that, like them, our hearts be free from doubt, bitterness, anxiety and despair and be filled, instead, with the joys You send us (even as we suffer) and with love, love, and LOVE.

❦ FOR PONDERING ❦

Have there been any widow saints whose stories you especially relate to? In what ways?

_____

_____

_____

_____

_____

_____

❦ PRAYER OF THE DAY ❦

Walk with me, Jesus ... (insert your own prayer here)

_____

_____

_____

_____

_____

_____

_____

BLESSED MARIE OF THE INCARNATION:
CONTEMPLATIVE MYSTIC

"I have been in great torment, imagining the pitfalls where you might stumble. But finally our gracious God gave me peace in the belief that his loving and fatherly goodness would never lose what had been abandoned for his love...."

Blessed Marie in a letter to her son

Marie Guyart was born in 1599 into a middle-class family of bakers in Tours, France. At the age of seven, she was greatly influenced by a mystical dream in which she saw the heavens open and Jesus come toward her in the form of a child. On fire with love for him, she opened her arms to embrace him. He took Marie in his arms and kissed her, asking if she would be his. She said yes.

Even though Marie was an unusually pious young woman, her parents thought that her very practical nature suited her better for marriage, and she accepted their judgment. She married a merchant named Claude Martin, who died less than a year after their son was born. She was eighteen.

With her fine business mind, Marie saved her husband's business and administered the affairs of other relatives, into whose house she eventually moved. Her most mystical experiences of Christ (including the Sacred Heart of Jesus), the Eucharist, and the Trinity took place while she was working on the docks alongside rough stevedores, watering the horses!

In one of her most pivotal mystical experiences, when Marie was only twenty-one, she recalls: "My inner eyes were opened and all the faults, sins, and imperfections that I had committed since my birth were shown to me in the most vivid detail. At the same moment I saw myself immersed in the blood of the Son of God, shed because of the sins which had been shown to me; and further realizing that it was for my salvation that this Precious Blood had been shed."

This experience, she later recounted, changed her "into another person — and so powerfully changed that I did not even recognize myself. My ignorance, which had led me to think that I was perfect, that my actions were all innocent, and that I was quite a fine person, was now unmasked and I acknowledged that all my righteousness was, in fact, only sinfulness."

Many mystical illuminations followed involving the Eucharist and the Trinity. Marie said: "I was united to him who revealed to me the divine mysteries by which I lived, and my soul was satisfied. ... I found my heart beating so strangely that I was completely powerless. Had it burst open I would have found consolation in death, united to him whom I could conceive and imagine only as love."

She made a vow of perpetual chastity, and by the age of twenty-seven she received graces that are sometimes known as "mystical marriage."

Although Marie loved her son with the greatest tenderness, she also felt an ever-growing desire to enter the religious life. When her son seemed old enough to be entrusted to her extended family, Marie became an Ursuline teaching sister.

However, Maria's initial joy about taking the vows of a consecrated woman were quickly overshadowed. She entered into a period of frightening darkness exacerbated by a fearful anxiety for her son, who remained unreconciled with her decision. So intense was her dark night that she feared losing her mind.

Later, when she departed for Canada as a missionary, there was a second – and far more difficult – parting. She knew it was unlikely they would see each other again. In one of her letters, she writes:

Your letter brought me so profound a consolation that it is very hard for me to describe it. All this year I have been in great torment, imagining the pit-falls where you might stumble. But finally our gracious God gave me peace in the belief that his loving and fatherly goodness would never lose what had been abandoned for his love....

You have been abandoned by your mother and your relatives, yet hasn't this abandonment been to your advantage? When I left you before you were twelve years old, I endured terrible agonies of spirit, which were known to God alone. I had to obey his divine will ... my heart was strengthened so that I was able to overcome what had delayed my entry into religious life for ten long years.... I foresaw that you would be aban-

doned by your relatives, which caused me a thousand pains; this, linked to human weakness, made me fear your ruin.

Marie's depressive state was relieved by a mystical dream in which she saw a land of great natural beauty, full of forests and mountains shrouded in mist. The picture she had seen became a reality when she journeyed to Canada to help Jesuit missionaries reach the natives of Canada and French settlers. However, Marie also experienced terrible disappointment when some of the French merchants corrupted the Indians with alcohol, thereby undermining their formation as Catholics.

Conflicts within her own community arose as well, and she grew melancholy, blaming the problems all on herself. What carried her through was the strength of her faith in Christ even in darkness and also her tremendous love for the primitive native children on whom she lavished tenderness for both body and soul.

Blessed Marie died in her seventies in her Canadian monastery, longing for the total union with her Second Bridegroom in eternity, of which her mystical experiences were such a foretaste.

🐚 FOR REFLECTION AND DISCUSSION 🐚

Though she was a saint, Blessed Marie struggled throughout her life with periods of great interior darkness. Frequently depression is attributed to ingrown anger or guilt ... yet this story offers another perspective. What can we learn from Blessed Marie's bouts of depression?

_____

_____

_____

_____

_____

_____

PSALM 46:2-7

God is our refuge and our strength,
an ever-present help in distress.

Thus we do not fear, though earth be shaken and
mountains quake to the depths of the sea,

Though its waters rage and foam and mountains
     totter at its surging.
The LORD of hosts is with us; our stronghold is the
     God of Jacob. Selah

Streams of the river gladden the city of God,
the holy dwelling of the Most High.

God is in its midst; it shall not be shaken;
God will help it at break of day.

Though nations rage and kingdoms totter,
God's voice thunders and the earth trembles.

The LORD of hosts is with us; our stronghold is the
God of Jacob. Selah

❦ FOR PONDERING ❦

How would you paraphrase this psalm to fit the circumstances of your own life?

"Thus we do not fear, though …"

_____

_____

_____

_____

_____

_____

_____

❦ PRAYER OF THE DAY ❦

Lord, I will not fear today, even … (finish your prayer here).

_____

_____

_____

_____

_____

_____

_____

WHEN CHILDREN LEAVE US

"The God of all grace who called you to his eternal glory through Christ [Jesus] will himself restore, confirm, strengthen, and establish you after you have suffered a little. To him be dominion forever. Amen."

1 Peter 5:10-11

The children of Saint Elizabeth Seton were more of a consolation than a concern, at least until they were older. Elizabeth had five children: Anna Maria, William, Richard, Catherine, and Rebecca; they were all very close in age, seven years separating the oldest from the youngest. Her eldest daughter, then eight years old, accompanied her on the voyage to Italy that ended in her widowhood. After her husband died, six months passed before she saw the youngest four children again.

Elizabeth wrote in a letter to a friend: "Once more to see my darlings seems to me more happiness than I dare to ask for — My William charged me always to make them look for him in heaven..."

Two of the daughters died before Elizabeth, cherished to the last moment in the arms of their beloved mother. Elizabeth worried a lot about her sons. They were good but not talented or ambitious. She had hoped one might feel called to the priesthood, but she would never press this hope unless it clearly came from God.

As is the case with so many Catholic mothers, and especially divorced or widowed, Elizabeth was terrified that once out in the world, following the completion of their formal Catholic education, her sons would fall into sin. "I have no earthly interest for them — only one point in view — their precious souls and dear Eternity," she wrote.

⬧ FOR PONDERING ⬧

"I have no earthly interest for them … [except] their precious souls and dear Eternity."

Is this how you feel about your family? Have you formally entrusted them into God's keeping?

_____

_____

_____

_____

_____

_____

_____

_____

In recent months you have had ample opportunity to experience firsthand how short the time is that we have to ready our hearts for heaven. What has this experience taught you, that you would like to pass on to your children?

Write about it here.

_____

_____

_____

_____

_____

_____

_____

St. Elizabeth Seton:
"I Was Never So Happy"

LORD, my heart is not proud; nor are my eyes haughty.
I do not busy myself with great matters, with things too sublime for me.

Rather, I have stilled my soul, hushed it like a weaned child.
Like a weaned child on its mother's lap, so is my soul within me.

Israel, hope in the LORD, now and forever.

Psalm 131

Right after the death of her husband in Italy, before becoming a Catholic herself, Elizabeth Seton attended every liturgy possible, for there she could shed tears unnoticed, the others being so absorbed in their own prayers.

Seeing the Blessed Sacrament passing under her window in procession, she was moved to think about the Catholic conviction concerning the Real Presence that she, as an Episcopalian, did not yet fully believe: "I face the full loneliness and sadness of my case. I cannot stop the tears at the thought, my God, how happy would I be even so far away from all so dear, if I could find you in the church as they do...."

Elizabeth Seton was very impressed by the fact that Catholics could go to daily Mass. When she became a Catholic herself, at her First Communion, she wrote to Amabilia Filicchi:

"God is mine and I am his ... a triumph of joy and gladness that the deliverer was come, and my defense and shield and strength and Salvation made mine for this World and the next ... now then all the excesses of my heart found their play and it danced with more fervor ... perhaps almost with as much as the royal prophets before his Ark ... truly I feel all the powers of my soul held fast by him who came with so much Majesty to take possession of this little poor Kingdom."

There were times when Elizabeth expressed fear about the future, with no clear path and many monetary worries. Her friend Antonio Filicchi told Elizabeth, "My little Sister, God, the Almighty, is laughing at you; he takes care of little birds and makes the lilies grow, and you fear he will not take care of you — I tell you he will take care of you."

In her journal, Elizabeth wrote: "My Saviour, My Jesus, hide me. Shelter me, shelter the shuddering trembling soul [that] lays itself in thy hand." And in a letter, she wrote: "I never was so happy — not in the brightest years of my life – and never experienced an enjoyment to be compared with a moment's Blessedness at communion."

She continues: "Look up, my soul. Fear not, the love that nourishes us is unchangeable as Him from whom it proceeds — it will remain when every other sentiment will vanish. And could we desire more than to draw continual refreshment from a stream so near the fountainhead — so pure so sweet a stream!"

It is in her moments of insecurity, however, that I find the greatest encouragement:

"... the most painful things in the order of His providence can increase our confidence and Peace in Him, since all will draw us but nearer to Himself if we only kiss His hand as that of the best of Fathers."

🐚 PRAYER OF THE DAY 🐚

Lord Jesus, with St. Elizabeth I pray: *"My Saviour, My Jesus, hide me. Shelter me, shelter the shuddering trembling soul [that] lays itself in thy hand."*

Thank You for walking with me these many weeks, especially in the course of this study. Thank You for the fresh insights that I have received, for the consolations I have experienced … and for the new friends I have made, especially among the widow saints.

Immaculate Widow, please pray for me as I continue my journey.

Widow saints, thank you for your blessed companionship!

APPENDIX A:
PRAYERS AND MEDITATIONS FOR THE JOURNEY

Are there any prayers or verses that you have found particularly
meaningful? Write them here …

_____

_____

_____

_____

_____

_____

_____

_____

_____

_____

_____

_____

_____

_____

_____

_____

_____

_____

Appendix B:
Index of Widows

The following is a listing of Widow saints:

- Saint Adelaide (931-999)
- Blessed Angela of Foligno (1248-1309)
- Blessed Angeline Corbara (died 1377)
- Saint Brigid (also called Bridget, Birgitta, or Brigitta) of Sweden (1323-1373)
- Saint Catherine of Genoa (1447-1510)
- Blessed Clare of Rimini (1282-1346)
- Saint Clotilda (474-545)
- Concepcion (Conchita) Cabrera de Armida (1862-1937)
- Blessed Dorothy of Mantua (1347-1394)
- Saint Elizabeth of Hungary (1207-1231)
- Saint Elizabeth of Portugal (1271-1336)
- Saint Elizabeth Seton (1774-1821)
- Saint Ethelreda (or Audrey) (died 679)
- Saint Frances of Rome (1384-1440)
- Blessed Humiliana Cerchi (1216-1246)
- Saint Jane (or Jeanne) de Chantal (1572-1641)
- Blessed Jane (or Jeanne) de Maille (1332-1414)
- Saint Jeanne de Lestonnac (died 1640)
- Saint Joaquina (1783-1854)
- Saint Jutta (died 1260)
- Blessed Louise Albertoni (1474-1533)
- Saint Louise de Marillac (1591-1660)
- Blessed Maria Domenica Brun Barbantini (1789-1868)
- Mother Maria Luisa Josefa of the Blessed Sacrament (1866-1937)
- Blessed Marie Marguerite d'Youville (1701-1771)
- Blessed Marie of the Incarnation (Acarie) (1566-1618) - All references to Blessed Marie of the Incarnation in this work are to the next one of that name with the last name of Martin and not Acarie.)

- Blessed Marie of the Incarnation (Martin) (1599-1672)
- Saint Matilda (895-968)
- Blessed Michelina of Pesaro (1300-1356)
- Saint Monica (331-387)
- Saint Paula (347-404)
- Praxedes Fernandez (died 1936)
- Saint Rita of Cascia (1381-1457)

Happy Married Saints:

- The Virgin Mary (wife of Saint Joseph),
- Saint Paula
- Saint Clotilda
- Saint Matilda
- Saint Jutta
- Saint Elizabeth of Hungary
- Saint Brigid of Sweden
- Blessed Jane de Maille (had a celibate marriage with her first husband)
- Saint Frances of Rome
- Saint Catherine of Genoa (her husband agreed to a celibate marriage after her conversion)
- Saint Jane de Chantal
- Saint Jeanne de Lestonnac
- Blessed Louise Albertoni
- Saint Louise de Marillac
- Saint Joaquina
- Saint Elizabeth Seton
- Concepcion (Conchita)
- Cabrera de Armida.

Reluctantly Married (either because they wished they could have been consecrated to Christ as his spouse, or because they rejected a particular suitor):

- Blessed Humiliana Cerchi
- Blessed Angeline Corbara
- Saint Brigid of Sweden
- Saint Rita of Cascia
- Blessed Louise Albertoni

Unhappily Married:

- Saint Monica (her husband, a pagan most of his life, was a worldly, ill-tempered man)
- Blessed Humiliana Cerchi (husband converted only on his deathbed, thanks in part to Humiliana's uncomplaining kindness)
- Saint Elizabeth of Portugal (whose royal husband was dissolute and jealous)
- Blessed Dorothy of Mantua
- Saint Rita of Cascia
- Blessed Marie Marguerite d'Youville
- Praxedes (pronounced *Prahk-SAY-dehz)* Fernandez

Widows with Young Children:

- Blessed Michelina of Pesaro
- Saint Rita of Cascia
- Saint Brigid of Sweden
- Saint Jeanne de Lestonnac
- Saint Jane de Chantal
- Saint Louise de Marillac
- Blessed Marie of the Incarnation
- Blessed Marguerite d'Youville

- Saint Joaquina
- Maria Domenica Brun Barbantini
- Concepcion Cabrera de Armida (Conchita)
- Praxedes Fernandez.

Former Sinners-Turned-Saints:

- Blessed Clare of Rimini
- Blessed Angela of Foligno
- Blessed Michelina of Pesaro
- Saint Catherine of Genoa.

Young Widows:

- Blessed Humiliana Cerchi
- Saint Elizabeth of Hungary
- Blessed Angeline Corbara
- Blessed Clare of Rimini
- Blessed Michelina of Pesaro
- Saint Jane de Chantal
- Blessed Marie of the Incarnation

APPENDIX C:
DEDICATED WIDOWS OF THE HOLY FAMILY

Dedicated Widows of the Holy Family is an association of widows with Mary, Exalted Widow as our model. We make a private promise not to remarry and to dedicate the rest of our lives to prayer, and building the kingdom of God in our families, society and parishes. We especially make ourselves available to our pastor for the needs of the parish. Rev. Ken Whittington of St. Charles Borromeo parish in Morganton, North Carolina, is our chaplain.

Background:

After trying many different ways to live as a widow, in 2007 at St. Charles Borromeo Parish in Morganton, N.C., I became a widow dedicated to the Lord. The little ceremony included a promise not to remarry and to live according to a rule I devised with the help of my spiritual director. The way of life that I followed for many years before 2007 has never demanded rigid obedience to the schedule then or now. Rather, it is altered as needed since my activities vary considerably.

🕊 Private promise never to remarry.

🕊 Simple life – giving to the poor or pro-life everything I don't truly need.

🕊 Daily Mass and frequent Confession.

🕊 Daily Rosary.

🕊 Chaplet of Divine Mercy.

🕊 Daily prayer from the Liturgy of the Hours and Office of Readings and other spiritual readings.

🕊 Silent prayer at Adoration in the Church or in my oratory at home.

🕊 Apostolic endeavors such as writing, speaking and teaching.

🕊 While not under strict obedience, I do consult my spiritual director whose advice is a great help to me.

❦

PRAYER OF DEDICATED WIDOWS
OF THE HOLY FAMILY

God the Father,
I offer you the rest of my time on earth
that I may serve with love
and come to eternal life.
May my husband be blessed on his journey in eternity
and everyone in my family be saved.

Holy Spirit,
comfort all widows,
especially newly bereaved,
and inspire each member of
Dedicated Widows of the Holy Family.

Jesus,
my bridegroom,
savior of my soul,
delight of my heart;
help me.

Mary,
exalted widow,
mother of the Church,
my model and intercessor;
pray for me.

St. Joseph,
protector of Mary and the child Jesus
and helper of widows;
guide me in the trials of daily life.

In June of 2007 it seemed to me that the Lord wanted me to form an Association of Widows. Such widows could live together but most would live in their homes and dioceses. With many practices individually discerned, in common being a Dedicated Widow of the Holy Family includes these commitments

🖙 A promise never to re-marry in order to devote ourselves to Christ and the Church. This promise is made with the permission of a priest (such a promise can be dispensed by any priest should you change your mind). Usually a priest will want you to spend a year or more making sure this is a good promise before the promise is formally made.

🖙 Daily Mass when possible and frequent Confession (once a month if possible)

🖙 Daily Rosary – 5 decades each day

🖙 Prayer of Dedicated Widows of the Holy Family *(Page 229)*

🖙 Quiet prayer (between ½ and 1 hour daily unless omitted for good reasons)

🖙 Simplicity of life as discerned by each member. All Catholics are called to live simply and austerely and to give generously to the needy. Our needs vary, however. One widow needs a house because of family. Another's simplicity of life would call for living in an apartment or room as near as possible to the parish. We give as much as we can to the needy often including the needy in our own families. Dedicated widows dress simply, avoiding luxury and styles that draw attention. We wear in a visible manner a crucifix at least two inches in length.

🖙 Acceptance of magisterial church teaching (including moral teachings of the Church as explained in the *Catechism of the Catholic Church*).

🖙 Service in the parish and the wider Church and society as discerned with the Pastor. Some ways to serve include

‡ Help with Extraordinary Ministry of Holy Communion at Mass or in visitation to the sick and homebound;

‡ Volunteer at hospice, Vincent de Paul, food pantries or soup kitchens;

‡ Participate in social justice work such as pro-life, economic reform, peace-making;

‡ Help with faith formation and other teaching roles;

‡ Join choir and other ministry in the arts;

‡ Participate in prayer groups such as Legion of Mary, charismatic prayer, secular (3rd Order) groups;

‡ Ministry to the grieving such as widow support groups.

Steps to Becoming a Dedicated Widow of the Holy Family

1. Pray and discern with your pastor or spiritual director about making a private promise not to remarry and other features of the common way of life.

2. Contact Ronda Chervin to arrange for on-going conversations and (if possible) a visit. (I live in an apartment with a guest room and bathroom available.)
   E-mail: chervinronda@gmail.com
   Street Address: 722 West Union St., Apt. F, Morganton, NC 28655

3. Apply for membership with a one-year period of mutual discernment.

4. Read my book *A Widow's Walk* (go to www.rondachervin.com or go to www.womenofgrace.com to order the new edition from Simon Peter Press. Also read more about different widow saints as in the bibliography at the end of my book. I also recommend my book *Called by Name: Following Your Personal Spirituality*. Check my website for ordering details.

5. Work out a way of life with your pastor or spiritual director. This should be similar to the one described above but may have variations to

fit your individual situation in life. Try it and consult with me as you work on it. Send me a photograph of yourself by computer or regular mail. This will aid me in my prayers for you.

6. After a year's time arrange a ceremony for your private promise. Let me know you wish to make a commitment to the common way of life of Dedicated Widows of the Holy Family by sending me a letter from your mentor (priest or spiritual director) simply stating that you are following the way of life of a Dedicated Widow of the Holy Family.

7. Pray about forming a group of Dedicated Widows in your parish or diocese.

Should there be a desire for such, I would be happy to offer yearly retreats for Dedicated Widows.

Note: Dedicated Widows of the Holy Family is not an alternative to Consecrated Widows. Check my website (www.rondachervin.com) under Options for Widows to see if this vocation has become more widely approved in your country. Dedicated Widows of the Holy Family has nothing to do with any plan for contemporary deaconesses.

BIBLIOGRAPHY

Angela of Foligno: Complete Works, translated with an Introduction by Paul Lachance, O.F.M. (New York, NY: Paulist Press, 1993).

Before the Altar, by Concepcion (Conchita) Cabrera de Armida, can be ordered from Sisters of the Cross, 1320 Maze Blvd., Modesto, CA 95351.

Louis Biersack, O.F.M. Cap.,The *Saints and Blessed of the Third Order of Saint Francis* (Paterson, NJ: Saint Anthony Guild Press, 1943).

Bonnie Bowman Thurston. *The Widows: A Women's Ministry in the Early Church* (Minneapolis, MN: Fortress Press, 1989).

Saint Catherine of Genoa: Life and Sayings, translated and edited by Paul Garvin (Staten Island, NY: Alba House, 1964).

Conchita: A Mother's Spiritual Diary, edited by M. M. Philipon, O.P., translated by Aloysius J. Owen, S.J. (Staten Island, NY: Alba House, 1978).

Nesta do Robeck. *Saint Elizabeth of Hungary* (Milwaukee, WI: The Bruce Publishing Co., 1954).

Francis de Sales, Jane de Chantal: Letters of Spiritual Direction, translated by Peronne Marie Thibert, V.H.M.; selected and introduced by Wendy M. Wright and Joseph F. Poer, O.S.F.S.; Preface by Henri J. M. Nouwen (New York, NY: Paulist Press, 1988).

Hands to the Needy: Mother d'Youville, Apostle to the Poor, by Mary Pauline Fitts, G.N.S.H. (New York, NY: Doubleday and Co., 1950).

Johannes Jorgensen, *Saint Bridget of Sweden,* translated by Ingebord Lund (New York, NY: Longmans Green and Co., 1954), Vol. II.

Rita: The Saint of the Impossible, by Jo Lemoine, translated by Florestine Audette, R.J.M. (Boston, MA: St. Paul Books and Media, 1992).

Marie of the Incarnation: Selected Writings, edited by Irene Mahoney, O.S.U. (New York, NY: Paulist Press, 1989).

Martin-Maria Olive, O.P., *Praxedes: Wife, Mother, Widow and Lay Dominican* (Rockford, Ill: TAN Books and Publishers, 1987).

Andre Ravier, S.J., *St. Jeanne de Chantal: Noble Lady, Holy Woman,* translated by Mary Emily Hamilton (San Francisco, CA: Ignatius Press, 1989).

Saint Elizabeth Seton, *Selected Writings from the Journal and Letters of Elizabeth Seton,* edited by Ellin Kelly and Annabelle Melville (New York, NY: Paulist Press)

Alice von Hildebrand, *By Grief Refined* (Steubenville, OH: Franciscan University Press, 1994).

M.V. Woodgate, *St. Louise de Marillac: Foundress of the Sisters of Charity* (St. Louis, MO: B. Herder Book Co., 1942)

ABOUT THE AUTHORS:

Ronda Chervin, Ph.D. is a grandmother, philosopher, author of numerous books about Catholic living, and a Dedicated Widow of the Holy Family. For more information about Ronda's books, audios, and videos, and other activities, go to www.rondachervin.com

Heidi Hess Saxton (editor of this edition) is an adoptive mother of two children and author of several books, including "Raising Up Mommy" and "Behold Your Mother." Her online outreach, the "Extraordinary Moms Network" is for women facing particular challenges in motherhood – especially adoptive mothers, single mothers, and mothers of children with special needs. For more information about Heidi and her writing, go to http://www.christianword.com.

*Johnnette S. Benkovic is the founder and president of Women of Grace® and Living His Life Abundantly, International Inc.®. She is executive producer and host of **The Abundant Life** television program seen on EWTN, and the host of the **Women of Grace Live** radio program heard weekdays internationally. Johnnette is the author of several books and the Women of Grace Foundational Study Series. She is a noted conference speaker, seminar presenter, and retreat conductor. For more information, go to www.womenofgrace.com.*